SENATORIAL
PRIVILEGE

The Chappaquiddick Cover-Up

by Leo Damore
CONDENSED VERSION

Cover photos by
AP/Wide World Photos
Black Star Publishing Co., Inc.

Reprinted and condensed by arrangement with Regnery
Gateway.

Printed in the United States of America.

1

THE FERRY AT EDGARTOWN, ON MARTHA'S VINEYARD WAS not scheduled to begin operation until 7:30 a.m. on Saturday, July 19, 1969. Nevertheless, ferryman Richard Hewitt beckoned a blue Ford waiting at the dock at 7 a.m. on board the *On Time,* a raft-like vessel that crossed the 150-yard channel to the island of Chappaquiddick in under four minutes.

The Ford proceeded on Chappaquiddick Road to a sweeping, hairpin curve, leaving the asphalt for the dirt ruts of Dike Road. A bumpy half-mile away was a wooden structure perched on pilings spanning a tidal pool called Poucha Pond. After negotiating the narrow bridge, the Ford discharged Robert Samuel, a high school science teacher, and 15-year-old Joseph Cappavella. Burdened with fishing gear, they continued on foot along a sand track between ranks of dunes to East Beach. After an hour of fruitless casting into the surf along that deserted stretch of shoreline, the two returned to the car. Samuel was contemplating fishing off the bridge into the pond when his attention was drawn to the glint of metal reflecting off a dark shape in the water ten feet away, on the south side of the bridge.

Looking closer through the ripples of tidewater, he discovered the shadowy outline of an automobile turned onto its roof, front end angled toward the bridge. Samuel made out the wavery numbers of a license plate on the car's inverted bumper.

Samuel and Cappavella headed at once for a cottage 400 feet from the pond. "Dyke House," read the printing on a mailbox beside the weathered shingles of the former hunting camp owned by Chappaquiddick resident Antone Bettencourt and leased for the summer to Mr. and Mrs. Pierre Malm of Lebanon, Pennsylvania. A self-possessed woman of middle age, Mrs. Malm was preparing breakfast when she responded to Samuel's knock at her door and received his report that a car was overturned in the pond. Then, Samuel and Cappavella returned to drop fishing lines off the bridge, oblivious to the car submerged on the other side.

Mrs. Malm telephoned the Island Communications Center maintained by the Dukes County sheriff's office at Martha's Vineyard airport.

At 8:20 a.m. a call from the Center was logged at the two-room police station located on the first floor of Edgartown's white clapboard town hall.

Policewoman Carmen Salvador relayed the information that an automobile was under water at Dike Bridge on Chappaquiddick to Police Chief Dominick James Arena. She said, "Do you want to send somebody over there?"

"No," Arena said, "I'll go."

Arena left the station with the cruiser's blue dome-light flashing. A sultry, clouding-up morning presaged poor weather for the second day of the Edgartown Yacht Club's annual regatta. For 13 years a Massachusetts state trooper assigned traffic duty and security at Boston's Logan International Airport, Arena was later attached to the Attorney General's criminal division, handling evidence of government corruption unearthed by the Massachusetts Crime Commission. "Because of my personality, and because I could handle people, I was running the jury room as far as witnesses were concerned to keep them happy and keep the lawyers happy," Arena said.

A newspaper story about a town meeting voting to raise the salary of its police chief to $10,000 in hopes of filling the vacant position prompted Arena to apply for the job even before he knew where that town was. The town, which he found on a map, would turn out to be

Edgartown, a picturesque former whaling port described as "tidy, shipshape and sparkling clean." In May 1967, Trooper Arena became Chief Arena, taking on a job which, in many ways, cast him as a virtual legate of the Chamber of Commerce: Policing the occasional excesses of seasonal pleasure-seekers upon whom Edgartown's tourist economy depended.

Pulling up to the ferry landing at the foot of Daggett Street, Arena asked Dick Hewitt, "You hear anything about an accident at the Dike Bridge?"

"Not until now," Hewitt said.

Chappaquiddick looked no more than two swimming-pool lengths away, the channel as close-quartered as everything else was in Edgartown, including the two car ferry that chugged Arena across. Apart from the modest swank of the beach club's cabanas, the island was a backwater of modest cottages midst groves of scrub pine and pin oak. In twenty years, the bridge at the end of Dike Road never had been the locale of an automobile accident.

Arena parked the cruiser beside the bulkhead. He asked the young men fishing off the bridge, "Is there a car over there?"

"On the other side," Samuel replied.

From the slope of the humpbacked bridge, Arena saw an automobile submerged but for rear tires beginning to show above the water-line. Gouges in a curbing of caplogs traced the path the automobile had taken before plunging into the pond. Arena judged the markings on the bridge's dusty planks, "Weren't really what you could call skid marks. They were more like scuff marks that probably were brought about by tires going sideways, sliding more than skidding across something."

Arena observed a woman approach the pond. Mrs. Malm was taking a look at the accident herself. She'd heard a car pass the house "going faster than usual" around midnight the previous evening, but nothing else.

Arena was amazed she had not heard the car hit the water. He asked if her husband had a bathing suit he could borrow. He followed her into "Dyke House" to change into plaid boxer trunks that, to his surprise, for he was 6' 4" tall and weighed 230 pounds, fit him perfectly.

Arena walked to the pond and waded in until the banking dropped off. He swam towards the car, encountering a turbulence of current. He dived underwater. He caught only a blurred glimpse of the automobile before he was dragged away by the inexorable force of an outgoing tide he estimated was running to a depth of six feet, because he could touch bottom.

Arena had a presentiment of dread: Whoever had driven off the bridge might not have escaped from the crushed and upended position in which the vehicle had landed and could still be trapped inside. Any survivor would have reported the accident by now; and there had been no report on the answering machine that recorded calls after the police station closed, or on the log Arena checked when he arrived at the station that morning.

Arena radioed the Communications Center from the cruiser. He told the on-duty dispatcher to have the police station send an officer, and the fire department's scuba diver to the scene.

Arena asked the two small boys standing near the bridge if they knew where there was a face mask he could use.

One of the boys said, "I think there's one in the boat." He ran to a flat-bottomed punt beached on shore and tossed a mask to Arena.

Arena dived into the pond again. The current repeatedly sent him out of control. He let himself be swept to the bridge pilings where he caught his breath; then swam back to the car. Hoisting himself onto the undercarriage, he found seating space beside the gas tank, there to await the arrival of help.

Arena had cut the inside of his big toe on some metal edge of the car, but he was too distracted to care whether the wound was bleeding. Word of the accident was bringing spectators to the pond's edge despite a light rain that had started to fall. After catching five bluefish, Samuel and Cappavella were packing up their gear, preparing to leave. Arena's activities in Poucha Pond had scared away the fish.

At 8:45 a.m., Arena recognized the blinking red bulb atop Edgartown Fire Chief Antone Silva's station wagon bumping down the Dike Road, followed by Antone Bettencourt's blue Jeepster. With Silva was volunteer fireman Laurence Mercier, the proprietor of an Edgartown grocery store, and police officer Robert Bruguiere. A "special" hired for the summer, Bruguiere was a teacher of business subjects at Natick High School. Arena told him, "See if you can get a registry listing for this license," and called out plate number L78 207 from the submerged car's inverted front bumper.

Bruguiere radioed the Communications Center to check the *Polk Directory* of Massachusetts registrations to find out who owned the car in the pond. Then, he drove the police cruiser to the beach side of the bridge.

Arena watched John Farrar adjust an oxygen tank across his back. Captain of the search and rescue division of Edgartown's volunteer fire department, Farrar had received a call at 8:25 a.m. to proceed at once to Dike Bridge on Chappaquiddick. Farrar left the Turf 'n' Tackle shop he managed in Edgartown for the fire station, where diving gear was maintained in immediate readiness. He was joined by Antone Bettencourt, a sprightly 70-year-old retired ferrymaster who drove him to the dock. Fire Chief Silva was waiting on the Chappaquiddick landing to help transfer rescue equipment to his cruiser. Farrar changed into a full diving suit en route to the accident scene, arriving there at 8:45 a.m.

Arena's attention was diverted by Bruguiere calling out information he'd received over the cruiser's radio. License plate L78 207 had been issued to Edward M. Kennedy, Room 2400, JFK Building, Government Center, Boston.

My God, another tragedy, Arena thought. His concern for the accident tuned to a higher frequency of alarm. But he had no time to ponder the stunning news that it was Ted Kennedy's car he was sitting on. Farrar was swimming toward him holding a safety line. He gave Arena one end of the rope, put an oxygen tube in his mouth and dove underwater.

When his mask cleared, Farrar saw in the wash of watery light he likened to the *sfumato* effect of a Rembrandt painting, an Oldsmobile sedan balanced on the brow of its windshield, tipped forward from the weight of the engine so that its rear end was tilted toward the surface. The car was facing the opposite direction it had been travelling before plunging off the bridge. Only speed could account for such aerial maneuvers, Farrar said later. "The car must have been going at a pretty good clip to land almost in the middle of the channel."

Farrar peered through the driver's side open window. It took 20 seconds for his eyes to grow accustomed to the gloom inside the car. The front seat was empty.

Farrar made his way to the back of the car, fighting a current he estimated was running four knots, hard to swim against for any length of time. Through the top right-hand corner of the rear window Farrar saw two motionless feet clad in sandals. So long as there was a possibility the occupant might be alive and breathing, he had to hurry and expand the air in the automobile and bring a resuscitator, if necessary.

Farrar moved quickly to the right side of the car. The rear passenger window had been blown out, shards of glass formed a ragged edge along the frame. Farrar thrust himself through the portal inside the car to his waist. Looking up, he found the body of a young woman. Her head was cocked back, her face pressed into the footwell, both hands gripped the front edge of the backseat to hold herself in conformity with its upholstered contours. It was not a position assumed by a person knocked unconscious by the impact of a crash, Farrar said. "If she had been dead or unconscious, she would have been prone, sinking to the bottom or floating on top. She definitely was holding herself in a position to avail herself of the last remaining air that had to be trapped in the car."

Farrar took hold of the right thigh. As soon as he touched the body, he knew the woman was dead; the flesh under his grasp was hard as wood. "Instead of life-saving, I was evidence-gathering," Farrar realized. "Because I was the only person who would be able to observe this situation, it behooved me to think about what I saw underwater to be able to report it."

Farrar rotated the body inside the car, a maneuver complicated by the victim's hunched posture and out-stretched arms made inflexible by *rigor mortis*. The body was "about one-quarter positively buoyant," Farrar observed. "There was still a little air left in her."

Farrar drew the body through the window head first. A gold chain clasped about the waist came undone and slipped off. He struggled to maintain his position beside the car against the current. Concerned he might lose the body when he swam to the surface, Farrar bound the safety line about the woman's neck. He tugged on the rope to signal he was coming up. Clasping the body over his head, Farrar pushed off. He broke the surface as Arena was gathering in the last feet of slack line. Farrar noted with satisfaction that the police chief's assistance was not required to bring the body up. The difficult recovery had taken him ten minutes.

The current took Farrar downstream toward the bridge. Holding the body in a cross-chest carry, he swam to the rear of Kennedy's car. For the first time in the several years he had known Arena as "a very placid individual, very calm and collected," Farrar observed him to be "excited and emotionally wrought-up." Arena had a quaver in his voice when he said, "My God, it's a body. Do you recognize her? Is it one of the Kennedy clan?"

"I haven't had a chance to see if I recognize her or not," Farrar said. He turned the body over in the water.

Arena examined the face for a Kennedy family likeness. Farrar observed "a great look of relief" on Arena's face before he said, "thank God, no. I don't recognize her. It isn't one of the clan."

Farrar undid the safety line. The victim's blonde hair was tangled in the half-hitch knots he'd tied. Farrar helped draw the body out of the water onto Arena's lap. Holding the corpse in his arms, Arena scrutinized the pale, lightly-freckled face, rigid in death. The mouth was open, teeth gritted in a death grimace. Pale eyes stared through partially-closed lids. She wore a long-sleeve white blouse, and navy blue slacks. There was a friendship ring on her left hand; two gold bracelets dangled from a wrist. "She appeared normal in the sense that there were no injuries that I could see," Arena said, later. "If she hadn't been wringing wet, it was as if she was about to go to work, or to a party, because everything was in place. Everything was buttoned right up."

Fireman Laurence Mercier called from the bulkhead, "Do you want the boat?" before pushing it out into the pond on a rope. Arena and Farrar placed the body across slat seats. The boat was drawn to shore. Passed hand-over-hand to the bridge, the body was placed on a stretcher in the back of the police cruiser.

Arena ordered Bruguiere to summon the medical examiner and undertaker, and have a tow truck sent to the scene. As required in all fatal automobile accidents, the Registry of Motor Vehicles had to be notified, too. Arena said, "And see if you can find out where Ted Kennedy is and get him down here."

Arena asked Tony Bettencourt to drive to the landing to wait for the medical examiner to come off the ferry.

Farrar dove underwater to retrieve the chain belt that had detached from the body. He checked the rest of the car. On the interior roof near the front passenger seat he found a workman's lunch pail lacquered with a *decoupage* of flowers, and fashioned into a handbag. When Arena opened it, water gushed forth a spillage of cosmetics and articles of grooming. A wallet contained a Virginia driver's license and a pass for the United States Senate, identifying Rosemary Keough of Washington, D.C. There were two keys for room #56 at the Katama Shores Motor Inn of Edgartown.

Arena radioed the Communications Center to confirm that Keough was registered at the motel. Minutes later, he received confirmation she was one of six young women who had occupied three rooms there since Thursday. None of the beds had been slept in the previous night.

Arena told Farrar to check downstream, "It's possible there were other people in the car. They might be in the pond someplace." He was walking off the bridge when the Depot Corner garage tow-truck pulled up with Jon Ahlbum at the wheel. The truck had emblazoned on its side panel: "You Wreck Em—We Fetch Em."

Arena didn't want Ahlbum to remove the car from Poucha Pond until registry inspectors arrived, he said. "They don't like it when an accident scene is disturbed before they can do their investigation." Concerned about the hazard presented by a growing crowd of spectators at the pond's edge, Arena changed his mind. The registry's office in Oak Bluffs was closed on Saturday. "I don't think we can get a hold of the registry today. You better get the car out as soon as you can and hold it at the garage." Arena added, "That's Ted Kennedy's car down there in the water."

"Gee, I just saw him at the ferry landing on the Chappy side," Ahlbum said.

"Oh, God. I better get a hold of him," Arena said.

Arena was walking down Dike Road when a Pontiac station wagon pulled up.

"Jim, can I help you?" Christopher "Huck" Look said. Look was a deputy sheriff and "special duty" police officer. A call to his cottage on Chappaquiddick suggested Look might be needed at the accident scene.

"You probably can help keep traffic away from the bridge," Arena said. "There's a car overturned in the pond. We're trying to find out if there's anyone else in it."

"I saw a car last night," Look said. "I hope to God that isn't the same one."

Arena was too preoccupied to continue the conversation and walked off.

Look got out of his car and watched the chief head for "Dyke House." Arena was going to call the police station to send somebody down to the ferry to locate Ted Kennedy.

2

ARRIVING AT THE LANDING ON THIS ERRAND AT 9:30 A.M., Antone Bettencourt addressed Dick Hewitt on the docked *On Time*. "Do you know about the accident? It's Ted Kennedy's car and there's a dead girl in it."

Hewitt nodded in the direction of a weathered ferryhouse at the landing. "Well, he's standing right over there with two men."

Bettencourt confronted Ted Kennedy. "Senator, do you know there's a girl found dead in your car?" he said. "Do you need a ride down to the bridge?"

"No," Kennedy said. "I'm going on over to town."

Bettencourt watched the *On Time* leave the landing for the crossing to Edgartown. Minutes later, the ferry was back. Hewitt made several round-trips during the next fifteen minutes. He observed Ted Kennedy and two other men "milling around" the ferryhouse. Hewitt wondered if the Senator knew about the accident. The same idea had occurred to Steve Ewing, the ferry's 16-year-old deckhand. "We realized by this time the Senator's car was involved in the accident," he said. "We thought he was waiting there for news."

Kennedy had boarded the ferry shortly after Ewing reported for work at 9 a.m. The Senator greeted the boy with a cheerful "Hi!" when Ewing collected three 15-cent fares. After the boat ride to Chappaquiddick the three men had gathered at the ferryhouse, which was furnished with benches and a public telephone.

Hewitt and Ewing walked off the docked ferry. At their approach, Kennedy edged toward a row of parked cars. He was within hearing distance when Hewitt called out, "Senator, are you aware of the accident?"

A tall man wearing glasses answered, "Yes, we just heard about it."

Hewitt and Ewing returned to the ferry. Kennedy and the tall man wearing glasses followed. "This time," Ewing noted, "Kennedy looked worried."

Steve Ewing's father was standing at the Edgartown dock. Vineyard bureau chief for *The New Bedford Standard-Times,* Harvey Ewing had heard about an accident at Chappaquiddick involving a member of Ted Kennedy's regatta party and had gone to the landing to cover the story.

It was 9:50 a.m. when he spotted Ted Kennedy on board the *On Time* bound for Edgartown. Ewing made ready to take a photograph, but before the ferry docked, Kennedy jumped off and was striding up Daggert Street at such a brisk pace, he walked out of focus. "That's why the picture isn't very good," Ewing apologized later. "Because I didn't get him full face coming at me off the ferry; I got him sideways."

Ewing wasn't sure why he had taken the picture. "I figured if someone in his party had been in an accident, it was a normal reaction for him to be over there checking things out, that he'd be concerned," he said. Kennedy looked "in fine shape," smartly turned out in light blue pants, white polo shirt and canvas deck shoes.

Ewing went to a pay phone at the dock to call Bob Hyde, his summer assistant. Ewing wanted Hyde at the accident scene while he maintained telephone contact with his paper in New Bedford. Ewing told him, "All I know is a car went into the drink and whoever was in it is involved with the Kennedy party. They think there's more than one person in the car."

Ewing was joined at the landing by Colbert Smith, assistant editor of the *Vineyard Gazette*. Boarding the ferry was undertaker Eugene Frieh, with the Buick station wagon he used as a hearse; his assistant, David Guay; and associate medical examiner, Dr. Donald Mills.

Mills had been alerted by his receptionist, Mrs. Thomas Teller, "Don't be surprised if you get a call to go to Chappy. I hear there's been a fatal of some kind over there."

Mills received the call because it was Medical Examiner Dr. Robert Nevin's day off. He left his office and drove to the ferry landing. Frieh invited him into the hearse for the journey to Chappaquiddick.

Mills observed a dozen bystanders on Dike Bridge. Wearing a bathing suit and a wet T-shirt, police chief Arena was entering "Dyke House." Arena used Mrs. Malm's phone to call the police station. He told Carmen Salvador to send someone down to the ferry to find Ted Kennedy.

"He's right here, Chief," Salvador said. "And he wants to talk to you."

"I'm afraid, Senator, I have some bad news," Arena said. "There's been another tragedy. Your car was in an accident over here. And the young lady is dead."

"I know," Kennedy said.

"Can you tell me, was there anybody else in the car?"

"Yes," Kennedy said.

"Are they in the water?"

"No," Kennedy said. "Can I talk to you? Could I see you?"

"Do you want to come over here?" Arena said. "Or do you want me to go over there?"

"I prefer for you to come over here," Kennedy said.

Not bothering to change clothes, Arena rushed out of

"Dyke House" to find a ride to Edgartown. He asked "Huck" Look for a lift to the ferry. Look didn't have his car there. Look approached Dr. Edward Self, standing near the bulkhead. A prominent New York surgeon and president of the Chappaquiddick Association of island residents, Self agreed to chauffeur Arena to the landing.

Arena was getting into Self's Land Rover when Bruguiere reported "Huck" Look had seen the accident car—or one just like it—"up at the corner" around 12:45 a.m. the previous evening.

Arena didn't give much notice to the report. Look was a year-rounder with a variety of part-time vocations, including off-season heating oil dealer. Arena would have plenty of time to question Look later. Right now, Arena was more concerned about this forthcoming interview with Senator Ted Kennedy at the police station.

Police officer Roy Meekins was waiting at the Edgartown landing, as he had been instructed when Bruguiere radioed to have a cruiser meet Arena there. Then Bruguiere greeted Dr. Mills. He explained that a young woman had been recovered from the overturned car in the pond.

Mills wanted the body brought to the front of the cruiser so as not to expose it to spectators standing on the bridge. The stretcher was placed near the cruiser's front grill. Mills uncovered a blanket to find "a well-developed, well-nourished, very attractive young woman" in complete *rigor mortis*. Her arms were stretched outward from her shoulders as if to ward off an assault; hands were frozen in a "semi-claw." There was a fine white froth about the nose and mouth flecked with a barely visible cobweb of blood that went directly to a capillary area on the left nostril. It was, in

Dr. Mills' opinion, "the characteristic foam that goes with a drowning case."

Mills ran his fingers through the wet hair for evidence of skull fracture, then the throat and neck. He unbuttoned the blouse to expose a lacy blue brassiere. He placed a stethoscope over the heart. There was no sound. He felt the rib cage; then tapped the chest, repeating the procedure with varying degrees of pressure. Each time, water welled up from inside the lungs, creating a splashing sound. The lightest pressure produced water from the mouth and nose.

Mills did not remove the brassiere to examine the breasts for injury. He slid the slacks over her hips, "exposing her enough to make an adequate examination," he explained. "I couldn't have removed her clothes without cutting them off because of *rigor mortis.*"

Frieh closely followed Mills' examination. As a mortician, "I more or less kept my eyes open," he said. Water seeped from the nose and mouth when the body was turned onto its left side, Frieh observed, "That probably came from her stomach."

"No, I'm pressing her chest," Mills said. "That's water from her lungs."

Mills passed his hands over the back and abdomen. He found no evidence of trauma of any kind. He diagnosed "an obvious and clear" case of drowning. "After all," he said, later, "the girl was found in a submerged automobile."

Mills overheard several bystanders speculating that the accident victim was a secretary employed by the Kennedy family. Mills ordered Frieh to remove the body to his funeral home, but to hold off embalming. In view of "certain non-medical factors and personalities" he had heard only as a rumor, Mills wanted to consult the District Attorney's office about a possible autopsy, he said. "If there's any Kennedy mixup in this, it's more than I want to handle alone."

3

IN FALMOUTH, JIMMY SMITH HAD WAITED ANXIOUSLY FOR further reports from Dick Ferry about the accident at Chappaquiddick. A second call confirmed a fatality was involved, but the identities of neither the victim nor the driver of the car were known.

Around three o'clock, Ferry called to say that Ted Kennedy had been identified as the driver of the accident car. Ferry didn't know what charges, if any, were to be logged against the Senator by Edgartown police.

Smith was stunned. He had spent most of his boyhood in Martha's Vineyard when his father worked for the phone company. He knew the island mentality well. "All my relatives over there hated the Kennedys. It was the old prejudice against Irish Catholics." Smith feared the consequences of a Kennedy accident occurring "in enemy territory."

Smith called Kenneth O'Donnell.

O'Donnell knew only what Smith had told him about the incident, he said. "I haven't been called."

The first thing anybody advising Ted Kennedy should find out was who the registry inspector handling the case was. Smith said, "It's a fatal, so you've got to have a registry guy there making out a report in addition to the Edgartown police. That's the key guy right there on any reckless driving charge."

Smith didn't know any registry people on Martha's Vineyard, but he did know Joe Greelish, who ran the

Hyannis office. It was no secret registry problems could be "fixed" on Cape Cod, Smith said. "Before Frank Keating came to town Falmouth lawyers couldn't tie their own shoelaces on traffic cases. If you had a license problem you gave Hank Jonah two hundred dollars and that usually took care of it." Jonah ran a bookie operation out of the Leeside Cafe in Woods Hole. Jonah and Greelish were very close friends.

Greelish was a savvy operator, politically well-connected. In September 1966, he had sought Smith's assistance in securing a postmastership at South Yarmouth on Cape Cod for his son. Smith recommended "a Democrat and a very deserving young man" to Ted Kennedy's office. Greelish had been badgering Smith about the appointment ever since.

O'Donnell told Smith to "keep in touch." If Smith couldn't reach him, O'Donnell suggested he contact his aide, Paul Kirk, Jr. Recently hired as counsel to a Senate sub-committee on administrative practices and procedures chaired by Ted Kennedy, Kirk was a natural pipeline for any information Smith might be able to provide from his strategic vantage point inside the district attorney's office.

Smith didn't call Edmund Dinis immediately. He thought about it for a while. He enjoyed good personal relations with the volatile and unpredictable district attorney. "He always acted like a teacher and a benefactor to me," Smith said. "He treated me like his kid brother." Despite his reputation, Dinis ran a four-county district with an able staff of assistants he left pretty much alone on cases. "That's why Dinis was re-elected three times," Smith said. "He ran a good shop."

When Smith finally did call, Dinis cut off his breathless recitation of the "known facts" about the Kennedy accident. "I know all about it. I've already been called."

But this demonstration of loyalty from the acknowledged "Kennedy man" on his staff put Dinis in teasing good humor. "We've got your buddy this time!" Dinis crowed. "We're going to get an indictment off a first degree. We're going to throw the book at him!"

Dinis let Smith dangle for a minute, then told him he was only kidding. "It's just a motor vehicles accident," he said. Dinis was content to leave the matter in the hands of Edgartown police, Smith reported to Paul Kirk.

Smith was confident the information would get passed along the Kennedy political network and eventually find its way to the compound at Hyannis Port.

But the Kennedy network had already been alerted to the crisis by the Senator himself. David Burke received the first call at Falls Church, Virginia, around 9:30 a.m. Kennedy was calling from a public phone at the ferry landing on Chappaquiddick to say he'd been in an automobile accident the previous evening. Despite the urging of his cousin Joe Gargan and Paul Markham, the accident had yet to be reported to the police. While he was fearful his car would soon be discovered in a tidal pond beside a bridge, Kennedy was still reluctant to go to the police.

The most admired of Kennedy's staff, Burke was a Harvard graduate and the son of a Brookline, Massachusetts, policeman. Burke's low, intensely urgent voice had battered down the last obstacle of Kennedy's resistance, making him understand there was no alternative but to report the accident as Gargan and Markham wanted him to. "You've got to listen to those two guys and report this thing. Go and do it right now!"

Kennedy asked Burke to locate Burke Marshall, "standby" at his senate office, and expect a deluge of inquiries about the accident.

Burke called the office to let press secretary Dick

Drayne know, "The Boss went off a bridge on Martha's Vineyard and one of Bobby's secretaries got killed."

Drayne was in the middle of a magazine interview.

"Anything wrong?" the interviewer asked.

"No, nothing really," a shaken Drayne replied, reflexively voicing the first in a series of evasions and half-truths he would be required to deliver about the accident in the next several days.

When Senator Kennedy called the office, Drayne could tell, "He was very upset, very depressed. But he could still come up with answers." Some of the answers were the stuff of which a major scandal could be made: The accident had occurred on a dirt road, late at night, following a party for a group of young women, and gone unreported for ten hours.

The Senator wanted no information about the accident given to the press. Drayne sat there all through the morning "waiting for the roof to fall in." By the time reporters descended on his office, "The story was on the wires about a former Kennedy secretary getting drowned," he said. "I knew what they didn't, that he was driving the car. And I could only give them what was already public."

Drayne was joined by Burke in the office to attempt to wrest some control over the exploding situation. The Senator had called several times from Edgartown's police station where he was writing a report of the accident. Kennedy wanted the telephone number of the accident victim's parents so they could be notified of her death. Burke came up with a number for Joseph and Gwen Kopechne in Berkeley Heights, New Jersey.

The Senator called Mrs. Kopechne around 10 o'clock. He asked to speak to her husband.

Gwen Kopechne sensed "a sorrow or sadness in the way his voice came over the telephone."

Kennedy reported, "Mary Jo was in an accident."

"Was it in a car?" Mrs. Kopechne asked.

"It was an automobile accident," Kennedy said. "Mary Jo was returning to take a ferry back to the mainland when the accident occurred."

Mrs. Kopechne asked if her daughter had been killed.

Kennedy hesitated, then said, "Yes."

The Senator gave her no details, Mrs. Kopechne said, later. "He just told me what happened and I broke down. I remember screaming: 'I'm alone here.' From then on, I don't remember anything. I must have let out some awful noises. A neighbor was outside hanging clothes. I must have let her in because I had the doors locked. She tried to get me to tell her what happened."

Burke Marshall was in Waltham, Massachusetts, that morning, preparing archives for a proposed John Fitzgerald Kennedy memorial library, when he got the call for help from Kennedy's staff in Washington. A self-effacing man of incorruptible character and strong moral convictions, Marshall had been selected by Robert Kennedy to head the civil rights division of the Justice Department in 1961. Marshall had defused an explosive racial confrontation in Birmingham, Alabama, by negotiating an agreement to provide a measure of desegregation, following a campaign led by Martin Luther King to end discrimination in department stores and lunch counters. Of him, Robert Kennedy said, "Burke Marshall has the world's best judgment on anything."

Marshall agreed "to help wherever I can," leaving at once for the two-hour drive to the Cape.

Marshall was already at the compound when Kennedy arrived from Edgartown "so upset . . . the question really was where to begin." Marshall found him "obviously disoriented but he appeared coherent."

Kennedy said he hadn't reported the accident for some ten hours because he was convinced Mary Jo Kopechne had somehow gotten out of the car and survived the accident. "I don't think he shook that idea for a while," Marshall said. After he was with the Senator for a time, Marshall came to the conclusion he'd suffered a "blockage," he said. "A lot of his mind wasn't accepting yet what was happening to him."

Marshall read over a copy of the Senator's accident report Markham brought back from Edgartown. An antitrust lawyer, vice president and general counsel for IBM, Marshall was entirely ignorant of Massachusetts criminal codes and motor vehicle statutes. He needed time to consult lawyers experienced in those matters.

Marshall had Markham call Edgartown police chief Arena to postpone release of the accident report. The statement had been made public, Markham learned; but Arena appeared loath to press charges.

Marshall instructed the Senator not to answer any questions publicly or privately about the accident. "The reason I thought he shouldn't make a statement to the press was that I didn't know enough about his legal situation," he said. In addition, Marshall was concerned that Kennedy could break down at a press conference, he said. He "truly did not know whether he might have a medical problem." Marshall advised Kennedy to see a doctor.

The Kennedy family physician on Cape Cod, Dr. Robert Watt, was summoned to Hyannis Port. The Senator told him he'd been in an automobile accident on Martha's Vineyard. There was a lapse in his memory from hitting Dike Bridge and struggling to get out of the submerged car. At the last moment, he'd grabbed the side of an open window and pulled himself out. He remembered diving repeatedly to get a passenger out of

the car, without success, going for help, and returning
to the accident scene. Again, efforts to rescue the passenger failed. Kennedy was driven to the ferry slip and
swam to Edgartown. Returning to his hotel room, he
had slept fitfully until 7:00 a.m. the next morning.

Watt's examination disclosed a half-inch scrape
above the right ear, a bruise with spongy swelling at the
top of the Senator's head, and a muscle spasm in an
area about the nape of the neck. He diagnosed: concussion, contusions and abrasion of the scalp and acute
cervical strain. His determination of concussion was
predicated "upon objective evidence of injury and the
history of the temporary loss of consciousness and ret-
rograde amnesia. Impairment of judgment and confused behavior are symptoms consistent with an injury
of the character sustained by the patient."

Watt prescribed a sedative to relieve the headache,
neck pain and generalized soreness Senator Kennedy
complained of. Later, criticized that sedation was con-
traindicated in cases of concussion, Watt said he'd been
misquoted, "But I wouldn't say he didn't get a sedative." Subsequently, Watt revealed he'd prescribed an
oral muscle relaxant, heat and bed rest and qualified his
diagnosis. Kennedy had sustained "a mild concussion,
was bruised and shaken up." He'd received a "blow on
the head, but he was all right."

4

EFFORTS TO CONCEAL OR "MISPLACE" INFORMATION ABOUT
the accident were building a momentum of reaction.
Much of the pressure was being applied to Dr. Mills.

Having relinquished the hour he customarily spent playing the organ at St. Andrew's Episcopal Church as a respite from the tensions of his practice so as to stay close to his office telephone, Mills was being challenged by reporters about the lack of an autopsy in the case. By 5 o'clock, Mills was "pushed to the point of irrationality and blackout as I tried my best to answer a barrage of questions. It got into such a chaotic state," he called George Killen to plead for help. "I'm being swamped with calls from newspapers all over the country," Mills complained. "What do I tell these people?"

"Tell them the girl died of accidental drowning and don't say anything else!" Killen snapped. "If they persist, slam down the receiver."

Killen was being hounded about the accident himself. One call came from his friend Frank Keating. A former assistant district attorney, Keating had worked with Killen at Barnstable courthouse. He wanted to verify reports of an accident involving Ted Kennedy.

"Yes, it's true," Killen said warily.

"And the girl was killed?" Keating said.

"She drowned," Killen said. Dr. Mills had called three times about the case. "I told him, 'If you want an autopsy let me know and we'll get a pathologist.' I left that strictly up to him. I asked if he was satisfied with the cause of death and he said he was."

"What a lucky son of a bitch Eddie Dinis is. He's got a United States Senator in the palm of his hand," Keating said. "He's got Teddy Kennedy for manslaughter."

Killen sputtered in protest, "Where's the manslaughter? Where's the evidence of negligence?"

"If Ted Kennedy was driving that car when it went off the bridge, there's no question of negligence about that, is there, George?"

Killen knew better than to argue criminal law with

Keating. "We aren't in it at all: Arena's handling the thing himself. It's a local motor vehicles accident," Killen said. "What do you know about this case?"

"I don't know anything," Keating said.

"Well, nobody does, at this point," Killen said.

Eugene Frieh was not surprised to hear from Killen. He was expecting the district attorney's office to order a "hold for autopsy" on the body of Mary Jo Kopechne. Instead, Killen wanted to know the scheduled departure time of the remains off the island, and verification that a blood sample had been taken.

State police had left a message at the funeral home that the sample would be picked up. After Killen's call, Frieh suggested David Guay drop the sample off at the barracks in Oak Bluffs. Guay turned it over to state trooper Richard Lucas at 7 o'clock. When he got back to the funeral home, Guay took a call from Dun Gifford, asking if there was anything more he could do to help with arrangements.

Guay told him, "No, everything's fine."

Gifford had spent a busy day on the island. He had seen the young women off on the ferry at Vineyard Haven with the assurance that he would escort the body of Mary Jo Kopechne to Pennsylvania the next morning. Before he flew back to Nantucket, Gifford reported the progress of his efforts to David Burke at Hyannis Port.

Leaving Dick Drayne to deal as best he could with Washington reporters flooding Kennedy's senate office with inquiries about the accident, Burke flew to Boston in the afternoon. A reporter on board recognized the pock-marked Burke and took the seat beside him. Reports of Senator Kennedy's accident on news wires were contradictory and incomplete, the reporter said. "Don't you think you should make some kind of full disclosure soon?"

Burke was offended by the idea. "I don't think we're going to do that," he said. "The Senator is not in very good shape. I'm going to go up there and maybe sit under a tree with him. And then we'll have to see."

But keeping a lid on the story was impossible. Before leaving Washington, Burke dispatched William vanden Heuvel to Berkeley Heights to hand-hold the grieving parents.

A former Justice Department lawyer, vanden Heuvel had traveled with Robert Kennedy during his presidential campaign. He arrived at the modest first-floor apartment in a two-family house too late to prevent the Kopechnes from talking to reporters.

A well spoken, good-looking insurance salesman, Joe Kopechne disclosed his wife had lapsed into shock after Senator Kennedy telephoned the news of their daughter's death. Ethel Kennedy had called. "She talked about faith, how it could help. She said, 'We will be at the funeral.'" No one at the Kennedy compound had volunteered any information about the accident. "Nothing was explained," Kopechne said to *Boston Globe* reporter Ken Botwright. "We still don't have any real details of what happened."

Kopechne didn't know what to make of a wire service story containing Kennedy's report of the accident Botwright read to him over the telephone. "We didn't even know she was with Kennedy—that kind of upset us. There we were, the last to know." The Senator had neglected to say he was the driver of the accident car when he called to report Mary Jo had been killed. Kopechne found Kennedy's evasiveness and lack of candor baffling. He had known about his daughter's trip to Martha's Vineyard with several other young women.

"We assume the girls went to the island to see the

Regatta with the Senator, but we're not certain. Mary Jo loved sailing. She went sailing at the Kennedy place on Cape Cod. Ted invited her up with some other girls right after Senator Robert Kennedy was killed."

Mary Jo was almost one of the Kennedy family. She was pretty well wrapped up with the Kennedys, Kopechne said. "Politics was her life. She didn't seem to have any time for anything much outside of politics. She wasn't engaged or anything like that."

"It was a good career, working with the politicians. It was what she wanted to do," Gwen Kopechne said. "She would have been 29 years old next Saturday."

Mary Jo Kopechne had graduated in 1962 with a degree in business administration from Caldwell College for Women, in New Jersey. After a year teaching at the Mission of St. Jude in Montgomery, Alabama, she joined the staff of Florida Senator George Smathers, then went to work in Robert Kennedy's office when he was elected to the Senate in 1964. In December she was hired by Matt Reese Associates, an organization that set up campaign headquarters for politicians. Reese confirmed, "She left on Thursday and said she wouldn't be back until Tuesday morning. She wanted to spend the long weekend on Cape Cod with friends she had made while on Bobby's staff."

Mary Jo had never worked for Ted Kennedy, Mrs. Kopechne said. "He just entertained them up there at Hyannis Port. After Robert Kennedy was killed, Ted Kennedy seemed to try to hang on to his brother's staff."

Mrs. Kopechne had spoken to her daughter on Tuesday, July 15, about the Regatta weekend on Martha's Vineyard. "We were talking on the telephone. I said, 'Honey, be careful of the water.' She said to me, 'Mother, you know me. I only like to sunbathe.'"

Mary Jo Kopechne had shared a house in Georgetown with three young women, among them Nance Lyons, an aide in Senator Kennedy's office. Her housemates were reluctant to talk about her. So were members of the Senator's staff who referred all inquiries to Dick Drayne.

That the Kopechnes had tipped off the press about a weekend party on Martha's Vineyard was bringing reportial furies down on Drayne's head. This was powder-keg information, bound to hurt the Senator if it wasn't defused fast. Drayne tried to lift the lid on the party just enough to remove some of the stigma beginning to attach to it. Mary Jo Kopechne was one of eight young women invited for a reunion of former campaign workers to a party in honor of David Hackett, Drayne explained. An aide in Robert Kennedy's presidential campaign, Hackett was in charge of the "Boiler Room" where trusted workers compiled intelligence reports on how delegates to the national Democratic convention intended to vote. "Ted came by to thank the girls for their work with Bobby. Then, this one girl had to leave. They were trying to catch a ferry when the accident happened."

Party guests had included the crew of the Senator's sailboat entered in the regatta: Paul Markham, former U.S. Attorney; Kennedy's cousin Joseph Gargan; and Jack Crimmins. Drayne described Crimmins as "a friend and long-time political aide" to Senator Kennedy. The presence of the Senator's chauffeur at the party begged more questions than Drayne had answers for. The most obvious one was: Why had Ted Kennedy driven himself to the ferry when his chauffeur was at the party?

Drayne suggested the Senator's wife had planned to fly to Edgartown on Sunday and sail back to the mainland with her husband. The truth was otherwise: Joan

Kennedy had not been invited to the Regatta weekend.

That Senator Kennedy made no mention of the party at Chappaquiddick during the three hours he'd spent at the police station "really bothered" Arena. "That's one thing I object to, that I had to hear about it from reporters. When I found out there'd been a party and everybody had left the island, I really got put on the spot."

Arena defended his ignorance as best he could. "I know nothing of any party. It's only a rumor," he told reporters. "Nobody has proven to me anyone connected with Kennedy was there, only that Joseph Gargan rented the house."

5

SHORTLY AFTER INSPECTOR HERBERT BURR CAME ON DUTY in the radio room at Registry headquarters on Sunday morning, he received a call to see if he could find a license for Edward M. Kennedy. When Burr found no record in the files, he went to the Tab Room. Here, licenses were key-punched on IBM cards attached to perforated renewal forms. Upon separation, the license was mailed to operators; the renewal card placed on circulating metal trays before being put in the Registry's files. The procedure took from two to six weeks. "When I looked in the trays, there were all yellow renewal cards there," Burr said, later. Among them was a license in the name of Edward M. Kennedy, valid until February 22, 1971. Burr had, on other occasions, found licenses that had been in the Tab Room for some time and hadn't been put in the files, but not for five months. Burr couldn't explain the anomaly in the report on the license check he made to Carl Catalano, chief of special investigations.

Having received confirmation of a valid license, inspector George "Red" Kennedy went to Edgartown police station, accompanied by Joseph Greelish. Greelish delivered the license number and expiration date to Arena.

Arena completed his citation. He was sending the "offender's copy" by registered mail to Ted Kennedy at Hyannis Port. In doing so, Arena wasn't following standard police procedure; such "tickets" were ordinarily delivered in person.

That he was seeking to prosecute the Senator for leaving the scene of the accident after causing personal injury marked the end of his investigation, Arena told a dozen reporters at the police station. From his examination of the accident scene, Arena was "firmly convinced" there was no criminal negligence involved. "But in the matter of the time period after the accident, there is in my eyes a violation concerning going from the scene, leaving the scene." That the delay lasted ten hours was not important, Arena said. "If he sat in his house for 5 minutes without reporting the accident, he was in violation of the law."

Reporters wanted to know if Arena had looked into the possibility the accident was related to drinking at a party prior to Ted Kennedy driving off Dike Bridge. Having been deceived about the party, Arena had not asked that question of the Senator, he said. "There was no other physical evidence at the scene that there might have been drinking. I'm not pursuing that line at all. I'm still standing on the fact that there was no negligence involved. I really believe the accident is strictly accidental."

Arena had no plans to question those who had attended the party. The only witnesses to Kennedy's conduct on the night of the accident had been Kennedy's friends. In Arena's judgment, none could be expected to contradict his account or say anything to worsen his situation—so he saw no point in questioning them.

"I'm firmly convinced the Senator told me the correct story. He impresses me as a Senator, and as a man who would tell the truth," Arena said. "I think the Senator was more than cooperative with me because he released a statement more openly than most citizens might. Most citizens would want to talk with their attorney first." Arena conceded he'd given Kennedy a chance to speak in private with former U.S. Attorney Paul Markham who accompanied him to the police station.

Arena was surprised neither Ted Kennedy, nor his representatives had called him to provide more details about the accident. "I wouldn't say I was left out in the cold," he said. "But I did expect some additional information."

So did reporters. Arena was not likely to be the one to provide it. Reporters liked Arena because he was pleasant and accessible. But the consensus was that Arena seemed incapable of hanging a rap on Ted Kennedy more serious than a misdemeanor traffic violation. Nor was he gathering around the accident to do much investigating, appearing more concerned with explaining away any possible wrongdoing on the Senator's part.

Arena thought the case so wrapped up he'd even disposed of the original police report. "It wasn't in Kennedy's handwriting, so I copied it and threw it away."

Weeks later, Carmen Salvador admitted she'd fished the document from a wastebasket to keep as a souvenir. Arena demanded the statement returned. "I felt it would be good for my files, because I figured I'm the only guy that's going to get questioned about this thing for the rest of my life." But even after it had been returned, the document proved elusive. "The truth is, one page of the damn thing did disappear again," Arena said. "I don't know where the hell it went."

Arena had to be reminded by reporter Ed Crosetti of *The Boston Record-American,* "Chief, you better talk to 'Huck' Look." Arena had neglected to question the deputy sheriff in the confusion of events on Saturday. Look's comments at Dike Bridge hadn't seemed critical. Whether the accident occurred at 11:15 p.m. as Kennedy said in his report, or after Look saw the car, didn't make much difference insofar as a leaving-the-scene charge was concerned. Arena said, "The question of time only became an issue after the press picked up inconsistencies in Kennedy's report."

A husky man with the high color of the outdoors, and a plainspoken, country-boy manner, Look was reluctant to retell his story officially for the record in view of the Senator's published account of the accident. Look regretted having blurted out information before he realized its significance.

Look had seen a dark car between 12:40 a.m. and 12:45 a.m., Saturday morning approaching the bend on Chappaquiddick Road at the center of the intersection of Dike Road. Arena noted, "He is positive there was a man driving and that there was someone next to him. He thinks there may have been someone else in the backseat but he's not sure." The car appeared "unsure or lost." Look stopped, and started to walk toward the car, but the driver had sped off down Dike Road.

Look's story sounded OK to Arena. "The thing that bothered me about it was, 'Huck' was so adamant about his time. I did believe he saw this particular thing, but I was between a stone and a hard place because I couldn't disprove Kennedy's time."

Look was more closely interrogated by George Killen and Bernie Flynn when the two detectives arrived in Edgartown around noon. Arena hadn't asked for their help. The chief had left the station, telling reporters, "It's my day off. I'm going home to my family."

"This was more a spectator thing," Flynn explained. "George didn't want us involved, but he wanted to know what was going on. Because if Dinis stepped in, our office would get the case."

Flynn and Killen made a formidable pair, at opposite ends of the police spectrum. Taciturn and rigidly principled, Killen was in austere contrast to the good-looking blond with a fiery temper, as likely to crash through a door as to knock. A tough street cop, Flynn was "like a dog in heat" when he sank his teeth into an investigation.

Killen had taken an instant dislike to the younger man when Flynn joined his office in January 1967, regarding him as "an angle-player and a wise guy." Flynn had few scruples when it came to beating criminals at their own game. Cape Cod was tame-stuff after violent, gritty New Bedford, upon whose mean streets Flynn had worked his way up from patrolman to captain of the uniformed branch. Flynn had cut a considerable law enforcement swath through the economically depressed former mill city, riddled with municipal corruption. Before moving over to the state police and leaving town, Flynn sent a former mayor to jail for taking payoffs, and made a host of enemies, not the least of whom was a prominent physician with whose wife Flynn had carried on a scandalous love affair. The doctor's political connections reached into the office of Governor John Volpe. Dismissal from the state police or banishment to some remote corner of Massachusetts was in the offing for Flynn, Killen confided to Frank Keating. "George told me the colonel of the state police was going to call Bernie in," Keating said. "And they were going to move him out, because of this affair."

Unlike Killen, Keating admired Flynn's quick intelligence and dashing style as a police officer, and so it was Keating who warned him of trouble brewing. Flynn used political connections of his own to head off a hearing and retain his plum assignment on Cape Cod. Outstanding detective work on several difficult cases over those two years had earned Flynn Killen's admiration; then ultimately, his trust.

Killen knew "Huck" Look as a reliable and responsible court officer from cases he'd prosecuted in Edgartown. Look agreed to accompany the police officers to Chappaquiddick to reenact his encounter with the "Kennedy car."

Look had worked as a special police officer at the Edgartown Yacht Club Regatta dance from 8 o'clock to 12:30 on Friday night. Brought to Chappaquiddick in the yacht club's launch, Look got into his car parked at the landing and headed home. He had seen the headlights of a car coming toward him near the curve at the intersection. "Knowing the road, I slowed down, because there's a sharp corner that people usually will cut too close," Look said. "I wanted to make sure I didn't get sideswiped." Look came almost to a complete stop. A black sedan passed in front of his headlights. "There was a man driving, a woman in the front seat, and either another person or some clothing, a sweater, or a pocketbook in the backseat—what appeared to be a shadow of some kind." The car went off the pavement into the private, dirt Cemetery Road.

By this time Look had proceeded around the corner a little bit, he said. "I observed in my rear-view mirror that the car was parked. And it looked like they were going to back up. I thought they wanted information, that they were lost or something."

Look got out of his car and walked toward the other vehicle. He was 25 to 30 feet away when the car started backing up toward him, tail lights showing all over the deputy sheriff uniform he was wearing. Look believed the driver must have seen him, as the lights glanced off the badge and whistle on his shirt. He started to call out an offer of help, but the car took off down Dike Road in a cloud of dust. He observed a Massachusetts registration letter "L", he said. "And I did sort of a photostatic thing in my mind that it had sevens in it, at the beginning and the end."

Look returned to his car. A short distance from the intersection he saw two women and a man doing a snake dance down the middle of the road, "like a conga line." he stopped to ask if they needed a lift. The tall girl of the trio said, "Shove off, buddy. We're not pick-ups." The man in the group apologized. "Thank you, no," he said. "We're just going over there to our house."

Look mentioned the "lost car" to his wife when he got home at one o'clock. "I figured it was a man and his wife arguing about what direction to go—that's the first thing that came into my mind," he said. "So many visitors come to Edgartown in the summer, you kind of get used to people getting lost."

Look wondered where the car was headed at that time of night. There weren't many places to go on Chappaquiddick once the ferry stopped running.

Given without hesitation, guile, or calculation,

Look's story was in clear contradiction of Senator Kennedy's report about the time the accident had occurred, and the wrong turn he said he'd made at the intersection.

If it was Kennedy's car—and every indication was that it was—to make a "wrong turn," a driver would have to ignore: (1) A directional arrow of luminized glass pointing to the left; (2) The banking of the pavement to accommodate the sharp curve; (3) The white line down the center of the road. To accomplish such a maneuver, a driver would also need to slow to a stop to make an abrupt 90 degree turn onto the unmistakable jarring ruts of Dike Road, a buckboard ride Flynn and Killen endured on their way to take a look at Dike Bridge, no more than a frail platform standing over Poucha Pond.

"Dyke House" was so close to the bridge, "There's no way you could go down that road and not see that house," Flynn observed. "It stuck out like a sore thumb." Diagonally across the road from "Dyke House," yet another residence was clearly visible from the road. Flynn counted two more houses Senator Kennedy had passed when he'd returned to the cottage after plunging into the pond. It took Flynn and Killen 23 minutes to walk the 1.2 miles from the bridge to the cottage, a nondescript house of weathered cedar shingles only 150 yards from the Chappaquiddick Volunteer Fire Station. A red bulb burned over the unlocked door of the cement-block fire station; a switch inside tripped a roof-mounted siren. Had the alarm been sounded, "I would have been there in three minutes. And my volunteers and half the people on the island would have shown up within 15 minutes," Fire Captain Foster Silva said.

Silva challenged Flynn and Killen when they came up

the flagstone path from a split-rail fence to the property
he was guarding from curious reporters and tourists.
Watchman for various summer residents and the Trust-
ees of Reservations that maintained a wildlife refuge on
the eastern shore of Chappaquiddick, Silva had let
himself in with a caretaker's key provided by the cottage
owner, Sydney Lawrence of Scarsdale, New York.
Learning of the accident Lawrence immediately went to
Edgartown and inspected the place on Saturday night.
He found it swept clean of any evidence a party had
been held there. Lawrence told Silva, "They were real
cute about that. I only found 8 empty Coke bottles.
Even the trash barrels had been emptied."

Silva lived less than 100 yards from the cottage. He
had no trouble remembering the party held there on
Friday night. He had watched television until 10 p.m.,
when his dogs started barking. "I went outside with my
wife to quiet the dogs and saw two, three cars at the
Lawrence house," he said. "There was a lot of singing
and laughing coming from the house. I would say it was
just a normal cocktail party. They were damned loud,
though."

Silva went to bed around midnight but couldn't sleep
with all the noise the dogs were making because of the
party next door. Silva thought the revelers were incon-
siderate in not lowering their voices after 11 p.m. "By
one o'clock I was pretty well damn fed-up with the
whole thing. It was a damn farce at that hour of the
morning. If they had kept it up any longer I would have
called the police."

Silva's son-in-law also described the party as "one of
those loud, noisy brawls" put on by summer people.
"There was yelling, music and general sounds of hell-
raising." The talk and laughter continued until 1:30
a.m., then quieted down. Silva's wife, Dodie, said,

"You could still hear people talking, but the noise level was not so bad. It was still going on when I went to bed at 2:30 a.m."

Silva hadn't known Senator Kennedy was at the party until the next morning when the accident car was hoisted from Poucha Pond. His wife recognized the automobile immediately. She'd noticed the car go by the house several times that afternoon, driven by "a middle-aged man with grey hair," she said. "I saw the same man driving the car after nine o'clock in the evening. He was heading towards the ferry."

Flynn was surprised at the modesty of a premises hired for "a Kennedy party." The living room-kitchen was panelled in knotty pine. There was a dining table and four chairs, a floor lamp, and a studio couch wrapped in flowered cretonne. A 9 × 12 Sears & Roebuck carpet filled the living room's entire floor space. A waist-high counter divided the living room from a gallery kitchen. Flynn found four packages of frozen crabmeat, butter, milk, and three bags of ice cubes in the refrigerator. A bathroom separated two bedrooms identically furnished with a varnished chest of drawers, a bottle lamp and mirror. A blanket was rolled at the foot of each twin bed, each so neatly-made Flynn wondered that they'd been slept in.

Silva pointed out a backyard building. "That's Mrs. Lawrence's studio; she paints there."

The studio was locked.

Flynn and Killen took a place in the line of automobiles waiting to board the *On Time*. The ferry was packed with visitors returning from Edgartown's newest tourist attraction. The traffic broke all previous records by more than one hundred cars, owner-operator Jared Grant revealed.

Grant had taken Senator Kennedy and a man he

didn't know to Chappaquiddick around 6:30 p.m., Friday night. He had operated the ferry until 12:45 a.m., when he made his last run to Chappaquiddick. Grant puttered around the boat for another half hour. "The reason I stayed was, it was too hot to sleep." He had observed "a lot of people in the area on the Edgartown side." Several youths were fishing off the dock; boats were running back and forth in the harbor, he said. "It was a beautiful night, very calm. The water was like glass."

Grant closed down at 1:20 a.m. He didn't recall taking Senator Kennedy to Edgartown. "I was dead certain I didn't bring him back until I got to reading the papers. He might have been on, I don't know."

The ferry could be summoned at any hour. "We come out for any legitimate reason," Grant said. "It doesn't have to be a case of an accident or injury."

Ferryman, Dick Hewitt said, "If someone wanted ferry service after midnight, they would call Jared's or my house. The numbers are posted on a sign on either side of the ferry." There was a public telephone inside the ferryhouse at Chappaquiddick. A bell was attached to the side of the building. "What people do is drive up to the ramp and leave their lights on; and we come across to get them. If you walk down, you ring the bell."

Hewitt was highly critical of Senator Kennedy's report of the accident. He said, "You tell me, is Kennedy finished? Or are they going to paper this over with $20 bills?"

6

WALTER STEELE WAS SUFFICIENTLY CALMED DOWN by the time Judge Clark and his son arrived in Edgartown for their Wednesday night meeting. Clark came prepared to do business. Arena had filed a complaint application charging Senator Kennedy with leaving the scene of an accident after causing personal injury. Clark wanted him to know, "There are technical defenses to this charge."

However, Clark had to be guided "by other considerations that transcend the usual criminal case," he said. He proposed Senator Kennedy admit to sufficient facts for finding of guilty. The procedure precluded a *plea* of guilty and said, in effect, "I don't want evidence of my wrongdoing presented as a case against me." The procedure required the consent of the prosecutor and the presiding judge.

The idea was so obviously a whitewash even Steele, timorous as he was about prosecuting anything more serious than a misdemeanor in a fatal accident, objected. "The judge won't go for it," he said. "And neither do I."

"There are defenses to this charge," Clark reiterated, implying a not guilty plea could be in the offing.

Steele wasn't fooled. "We've got enough to hook him in court," he said.

For the sake of argument, Clark said, "If we pleaded guilty, what would you recommend to the judge?"

Steele would recommend a suspended sentence for any first offender on a leaving the scene complaint, he said. "A suspended sentence would be fair to everybody."

Clark wanted "an assurance" Judge Boyle would go along.

You could never be sure about anything with Boyle,

Steel said. "You'll get a fair shake before this guy. He won't be influenced by the press, by Kennedy or anybody else. He goes strictly by the book."

Clark couldn't commit his client to anything so tentative. He wasn't a free agent; another attorney was in charge of the case. Clark had to clear everything first. Stephen Smith and Ted Sorensen had the most to say about the Senator's defense, he said. "They're calling the shots." Clark had to return to Hyannis Port before anything in the way of a plea could be decided.

That a suspended sentence could be forthcoming because Senator Kennedy was a first offender wasn't as comforting a resolution of the case to Clark as it was to Arena and Steele, because he knew what they did not: Kennedy had never been involved in a hit-and-run accident before, but there was a record of serious traffic violations. Their nature formed a pattern of deliberate and repeated negligent operation. Particularly bothersome to Clark was a June, 1958 conviction for "reckless driving."

The offenses in Virginia had occurred on Ted Kennedy's Massachusetts driver's license. But neither the Registry of Motor Vehicles in Boston nor the office of probation in Cambridge had any record of the out-of-state convictions when Clark checked with that agency. Though "clean" on the record, there was always the chance the press might rediscover the ten-year-old history of Kennedy's reckless driving and jeopardize his first offender status in Edgartown court, should a plea of guilty be made.

The technical defenses Clark threatened Arena and Steele with were: The vagueness of the statute as it pertained to reporting a one-car-accident; the constitutional issue of self-incrimination through the statement Kennedy left with Edgartown police; and, a medical defense of shock."

But the body of documentation gathered from the Senator's various examinations and treatment had undercut the medical argument. Instead, that body of evidence indicated Kennedy had not been seriously injured in the accident, but had suffered a slight concussion, a bump on the head, a scratch behind the ear, and a stiff neck. No medical evidence supported a diagnosis of shock. Nor did Kennedy's behavior at the Shiretown Inn the next morning reflect the condition. According to Arena, the Senator had looked "depressed, but physically OK," at the police station.

A not guilty plea required a trial open to the press and public, cross-examination of the Senator and the presentation of evidence against him. All those who had attended the party could be subpoenaed and made to testify. Deputy Sheriff Christopher Look was scheduled to be a witness to enter into evidence the controversial question of the time the accident had taken place. Look's observations that the driver appeared "lost" and "confused" could provoke inferences of impairment, such as drunk-driving, although neither Steele nor Arena had drawn that conclusion from Look's information.

Look's story "disturbed" other lawyers, McCarron said. "They were upset about it. The time difference was baffling to everybody." McCarron talked to Look himself and believed he had seen the car an hour and a half after Ted Kennedy said the accident happened. But McCarron wasn't concerned about the discrepancy. "I didn't think it would take that much for Senator Kennedy to conform his story on the question of time with 'Huck' Look's."

Despite the peril he could be placed in by his traffic record, Senator Kennedy might be wiser to take his

chances with a guilty plea to leaving the scene rather
than expose himself to more serious charges of driving
to endanger and, possibly, manslaughter, as a result of
more information coming out of a trial to defend a
misdemeanor.

As to manslaughter, the rule in Massachusetts was
clear: "Any person who wantonly or in a reckless or
grossly negligent manner did that which resulted in the
death of a human being was guilty of manslaughter,
although he did not contemplate such a result." Negligence in exposing another to injury by doing an act,
supplied all the intention the law required to make a
defendant responsible for the consequences.

A further manslaughter charge possibility had developed from John Farrar, the Edgartown fire department
scuba diver. In a number of interviews, Farrar repeatedly expressed the opinion that Mary Jo Kopechne
might have lived for some time underwater by breathing
a bubble of trapped air, and that she could have been
saved if rescue personnel had been promptly called to
the scene of the accident.

As a result of the famous Coconut Grove night club
fire in Boston in 1942, the Massachusetts Supreme
Judicial Court had broadened "wanton and reckless
conduct" to consist of "an intentional failure to take
such care in disregard of the probable harmful consequences." In upholding the guilty verdict of manslaughter brought against Barnett Welansky, owner of
the nightclub, for failing to keep his establishment safe
for patrons, the court had ruled failure to do an act
was as culpable as driving an automobile or acciden-
tally discharging a firearm. "Grave danger to others
must have been apparent, and the defendant must
have chosen to run the risk rather than alter his conduct, so as to avoid the act or omission which caused

the harm." Even a defendant "so stupid or heedless" not to have recognized the danger, could not escape the imputation of "wanton or reckless conduct in his dangerous act or omission."

If Senator Kennedy's failure to secure rescue assistance had contributed to the death of Mary Jo Kopechne, his omission to act was negligent. He was liable for prosecution under the *Welansky* decision. That was, in fact, the major legal prop under which District Attorney Edmund Dinis had successfully prosecuted for involuntary manslaughter in 1967 a Christian Scientist for failing to provide medical treatment for a child who had died of pneumonia.

Senator Kennedy confronted a legal dilemma: A not guilty plea required a trial, which could uncover damaging evidence against him. A guilty plea avoided a public inquisition and further revelations of wrong-doing, but made him liable to a possible jail term and provided an admission on the record that was one element required to prove manslaughter, should that charge be subsequently brought against him under *Welansky*.

If the hardest decision was what plea to make, Kennedy also faced the increasingly urgent need for a statement of explanation about the accident.

Kennedy's dependence upon speechwriters was legendary. In the preparation of a speech, most politicians briefed their writers before a draft was written. But Kennedy's writers completed a draft, then entered into discussion, during the course of which he was "usually receptive to other people's suggestions." Kennedy had assigned others to compose the famous eulogy delivered at his brother Robert's funeral. One of the speechwriters, "Felt pretty funny about it. Because, how could we know what he felt about his brother? He just said write something on the theme of love. I thought maybe that was one speech he shouldn't have asked us to write."

But composing any explanations of the Senator's accident at Chappaquiddick required a legal and verbal dexterity to explain away the ten hours it had taken for authorities to be notified. That task was assigned to Ted Sorensen, the literary light of the Kennedy White House.

Honored four days before the accident by the University of Nebraska as "a graduate having influenced national affairs and life more than any other living Nebraskan," Sorensen arrived at the compound, "full of brooding reproach for what Ted's mischief was going to do to the legacy."

Sorensen could hardly conceal his distaste for the whole affair. When Senator Kennedy called upon him to give legal counsel, "I responded to the call," Sorensen said, but he thought Kennedy's action at the time of pressure was indefensible. "The presence of a girl in his car and liquor at the party fanned the flames of ugly suspicion and wild speculation about his motivations for not going to the police immediately." Sorensen found it difficult, "To suspend my own moral judgments in working on a matter of that kind. And I therefore was insistent that whatever he said to the public, it did not contain misstatements of facts."

Sorensen consulted Gargan, "about certain things he was not aware of, that he wanted to make certain about." Gargan confirmed the rescue efforts he and Paul Markham had undertaken at Dike Bridge, his urging that the accident be reported, and Ted Kennedy's "impulsive dive" into the Edgartown ferry channel. Gargan said nothing about the alternative plans for reporting the accident Kennedy had proposed or Kennedy's suggestion that it was Mary Jo Kopechne who drove the accident car.

As the crisis passed into a fifth day of silence, editorial and political heat intensified. A leading Democrat, critical of Kennedy's behavior since the accident, suggested, "He can't let this thing deteriorate. I can't help but think he's been badly hurt. He may be able to come back if he's got some answers."

Reported under sedation, "still suffering from the traumatic shock of not rescuing Mary Jo Kopechne—a girl he hardly knew—from the car," Kennedy had made no decision to delegate a spokesman with authority to make statements or answer questions. It was unlikely the Senator would reveal more information about the accident before his court appearance, an aide said. Any comment might have a "prejudicial effect" on the hearing scheduled for Monday.

But the change in editorial winds brought increasingly strident demands for complete disclosure of the accident. Kennedy's report to Edgartown police was woefully inadequate. "Worse, there are good reasons to doubt that it is even accurate," *The Washington Post* charged. If, *The Post* said, Kennedy remained silent, he could expect not only honest doubts to remain about his post-accident behavior, "but also the bitter whispering campaign that has already begun. The talk will go on amplified about the initial timidity of the police and how the Kennedys managed that; about the drinking and the calls to lawyers and the various damaging versions of what actually transpired that night." Saying nothing would do Kennedy grave harm, "Which is why he would be better advised to get the politics out of it and clear up the record of this tragic affair."

"To end speculation and rumor that was vilifying the Senator's reputation and undermining public confidence in our law enforcement system," *The Boston Record-American* suggested it was "appropriate and essential in the interests of justice that an inquest be held into the death of Mary Jo Kopechne."

7

THE GROWING CLAMOR FOR MORE INFORMATION FOUND AN echo when, for the first time, Dukes County Medical Examiner Robert Nevin made a public statement that the circumstances attending the death of Mary Jo Kopechne warranted an autopsy. "We don't know if the girl died of a heart attack, a stroke, or from drowning," he said. Nevin said he would have asked the State Police to send a pathologist to Edgartown. "I wouldn't have let that autopsy go. I would have gone to Washington, if I had to. It wasn't too late when Dr. Mills learned the entire story around 2:30 p.m. The corpse had been embalmed, the presence of formalin couldn't change the picture."

Mills had performed his function of medical examiner by satisfying himself there was no evidence of foul play in the death, Nevin said. "But the point is that there are so many nasty questions, it would have been a kindness to Senator Kennedy to have an autopsy—so that all the nasty questions could be answered."

An autopsy could still be possible, Nevin said. "The order could come from the district attorney."

Dinis passed the buck. He would have preferred an autopsy be performed, he said. But it was up to Dr. Mills whether to order one or not. District attorneys rarely became involved in automobile accident cases, Dinis said. "In my 11 years as a district attorney, we've never investigated a motor vehicles accident."

Arena had reported the accident to him, "And then
for some reason bypassed me and contacted State
Police Lieutenant Killen." Walter Steele hadn't invited
Dinis to participate either. "For some reason they are
not desirous to get me into the case at all and I can't
understand why." With newspaper reports indicating
other charges could be brought in the case, "It would
seem to me the more manpower the better," Dinis said.
"It is an extraordinary investigation and unusual. They
are in the position where, if the case begins to crumble,
people will start talking."

By his attack on Edgartown authorities, Dinis was
hoping to deflect criticism about his office remaining
aloof from the case. Dinis had shown no eagerness to
become involved. In fact, Dinis protested that he
wouldn't step into the Kennedy accident case unless
specifically asked to do so by Edgartown authorities.

That Dinis had known about Senator Kennedy's
involvement in the accident by noon on Saturday and
not called for an autopsy was defended by Assistant
District Attorney Armand Fernandes. "You're saying
that since Dinis was factually aware at noon, that he
was legally aware for purpose of intervening. I say no,
no, no. You're saying he was supposed to change his
opinion right away in Senator Kennedy's case, whereas
with Joe Blow he wouldn't."

Dinis' office announced the district attorney "would
not be available for any further comment on this
matter."

That it was not customary for the district attorney's
office to become involved in motor vehicle accidents
came as news to Jimmy Smith. In February, Smith had
tried a hit-and-run accident on a direct indictment for
involuntary manslaughter. "I got hung with it because
the guy involved was a New Bedford fireman and a

former high school star athlete," Smith said. "No other assistant wanted the case. It was kicking around the office waiting to be tried for months."

The lack of information about the Kennedy accident was "deeply troubling," Dinis said, when he called Smith to complain of the inept handling of the situation by the Senator and his advisers. "Where's all this Kennedy expertise? Where are all the pros? Can you imagine them just letting this thing ride?"

Smith could only agree. With nothing coming out of the compound, Dinis' position was growing untenable. Smith wasn't concerned about the district attorney's office entering the case, "So much as the political time-bomb of no action on this thing. The beauty of the Kennedys earlier was that they acted, they didn't react. But this was a nonaction. All they had to do was come up with some answers. The longer it waited, and they couldn't, the worse it got."

The whole reaction of the parties was creating the suspense and mystery about the accident, whether it was intentional or not, Smith told Warren O'Donnell.

O'Donnell was grim, "Because of what was going on at Hyannis Port," Smith said, later. "Because Kenneth was being frozen out. They were giving out his name as being there as an adviser to make it look like all the old Kennedy hands were rallying around, hoping that meant to people that Teddy couldn't be guilty of anything serious—but that wasn't working at all."

O'Donnell thought Ted Kennedy was "screwing up" by delaying a public explanation of the accident. He had had direct experience with an earlier and notorious occasion when Ted had gotten himself in trouble. O'Donnell had arranged for his Harvard roommate, Bill Frate, to take a Spanish examination in Kennedy's stead. When Frate got caught, he and Ted Kennedy had been expelled for cheating. Warren called his brother.

In the midst of preparing John Kennedy's campaign against Henry Cabot Lodge, Kenneth O'Donnell told Ted Kennedy to pack his bags, but not to leave the dormitory until he received further instructions.

When the telephone rang, Warren recognized the voice demanding to speak to Ted as former Ambassador Joseph P. Kennedy.

"You're in the army. Report to Fort Dix at eight o'clock tomorrow morning!" the Ambassador announced, then hung up. O'Donnell swore it was "the real story" of the famous cheating episode.

Ted Kennedy had denied there was anything unusual about his interrupted education at Harvard. The Korean war was on and he thought it was "a good time to get my service over." Kennedy had served as an infantryman assigned to military police honor guard at SHAPE headquarters in Paris. A curtain of secrecy had enveloped the incident until 1962 when Boston *Globe* reporter Robert Healy discovered the story. Kenneth O'Donnell had participated in White House conferences seeking to persuade Healy not to release the information as a news story. A compromise had allowed Ted Kennedy to confess the incident, with a statement of contrition. The public had been forgiving of the "schoolboy prank," and the incident was defused as an issue in the election.

That wasn't going to be possible with the accident at Chappaquiddick, Warren O'Donnell said. Jack wasn't in the White House, and Bobby was dead. Whatever happened at Chappaquiddick was bound to come out. Attempts to "manage" the crisis were so blatant, nobody was going to believe anything but a complete disclosure.

Smith was worried the pressure on the district attorney's office was starting to tell. Reluctant as Dinis was to do anything, Smith said, "he can't duck the case forever."

On Thursday morning—now six days after the accident—Dinis called Dr. Donald Mills to ask, "I don't think an autopsy was necessary, do you?"

Surprised to hear Dinis mention autopsy for the first time, Mills said, "I really agree. I'm sticking to my guns on that."

Mills wanted the district attorney's office to issue an official statement about the accident. That way, he would be spared having to reiterate the known facts of the case to reporters who were continuing to pester him about the lack of an autopsy, and Mary Jo Kopechne's blood alcohol test figure.

Dinis was staying out of the case, he said. "I don't want another Lee Harvey Oswald affair. If I get involved, it's going to stir up a big Roman holiday in Edgartown. We don't want that; so we'll let Arena handle it."

Under pressure from reporters, Mills released the blood-alcohol test figure of .09%. He characterized it as "a very modest, very slight" level of alcohol in Mary Jo Kopechne's blood, an interpretation that immediately was challenged by other medical authorities.

8

BECAUSE THE SENATOR'S ADDRESS WAS REGARDED AS A news story, all three television networks donated 15 minutes of prime time to the broadcast. Boston's WHDH-TV was selected to originate the program, an arrangement made with Harold Clancy, general manager of the station and publisher of the affiliated *Boston Herald Traveler.* Clancy was spotted on board the *Marlin* in the zoom lens of a photographer standing at the periphery of the compound, one of a crew of reporters who jeered at the huge remote truck emblazoned with Channel 5's logo that was waved through the checkpoint on Scudder Avenue.

Among reporters who had stood a week's vigil waiting the release of a statement regarding the accident was *Herald Traveler* stringer, Francis Broadhurst. Learning WHDH had been chosen to provide the "feed" for the broadcast, Broadhurst proposed he masquerade as a member of the television crew to observe first-hand the speech and write a background story. Broadhurst was outraged when Clancy vetoed the idea. "I was pretty disillusioned that the Kennedys could exercise so much control over the press," he said. No reporter was to be allowed inside the house. The Senator wasn't going to answer any questions after his speech.

Following the remote truck in a small van was audio technician Don Moore. Assigned a crew to provide live coverage of the Miss Massachusetts beauty pageant in Attleboro, Moore had been chosen as part of a crew of five and told, "You're going to Hyannis Port."

Facilities for the broadcast were to be set up at the Senator's house. Moore drove to the causeway at Squaw Island, got out of the van and measured the distance between two entrance pillars. The remote truck couldn't get through. The location of the speech was moved to the home of Ambassador Joseph P. Kennedy.

The remote truck was proceeding down Marchand Lane, used by the Kennedy family and other residents, when a highly agitated man ran out of an adjacent house, demanding the caravan stop. He told director

Bob Kincaid, "You see those overhanging branches of that tree on my property?" If one leaf falls, I'm suing Channel 5 for damages!"

To assuage the irate neighbor, Kincaid stationed two crew members on top of the remote truck to divert branches from its path. Despite such precautions, Moore observed one leaf disengage. Kincaid was able to distract the tree-owner's attention as the leaf fell earthward. When it was within reach, Moore grabbed it and stuck it in his pocket.

While some facilities existed from previous television coverage originating from the compound, it was a race against time to install a hookup of television lines to deliver picture and sound beamed from Cape Cod via Providence, Rhode Island, to New York, where networks would distribute the program nationwide at 7:30 p.m., when the Senator was scheduled to deliver his speech.

At 7:20 p.m., the crew got a picture. Five minutes later the audio came in. Moore was asked by CBS for a microphone test.

CBS was in the midst of broadcasting the Nightly News with Walter Cronkite. The program featured an interview with Dr. Donald Mills conducted by correspondent Ben Silver, during which the medical examiner revealed the decision not to perform an autopsy on Mary Jo Kopechne had been "jointly made" with the district attorney's office.

At the interview's conclusion, Mills received a telephone call from Edmund Dinis. He said, "Mills, you let me down by not ordering an autopsy."

"He started to scream over the telephone about what a liar I was, how incompetent I was, and worse," Mills recalled. "When he launched into a personal attack, my wife picked up the extension phone and screamed right back at him. I will not give you exactly what he said, but he was unpleasant, quite impolite and he hung up the receiver in my face."

A light layer of pancake makeup was applied to the Senator's face to dull a surface reflection of lights. Kennedy asked his mother to join Stephen Smith and his sisters Jean and Patricia, in a room off the library to watch the speech on television. Joan Kennedy was more persistent in her attentions until she was ordered from the room by a short-tempered and tense Senator Kennedy as time for the broadcast drew close.

Kennedy took a place behind a desk. The desk and chair had been built up, using books as support blocks, so that the cameras were at eye-level, to give a more natural angle when Kennedy delivered his speech.

Kincaid was directing operations from the remote truck outside. Two cameramen were on the floor with Moore. At 7:30 p.m., Channel 5 newscaster Jack Hynes announced Senator Kennedy's talk was being produced by WHDH-TV Boston.

On cue from Moore, Kennedy began reading from a manuscript gripped tightly in his hands:

My fellow citizens:

I have requested this opportunity to talk to you, the people of Massachusetts, about the tragedy which happened last Friday evening.

This morning I entered a plea of guilty to the charge of leaving the scene of an accident. Prior to my appearance in court it would have been improper for me to comment on these matters, but tonight I am free to tell you what happened and to say what it means to me.

On the weekend of July 18th, I was on Martha's Vineyard Island participating with my nephew, Joe Kennedy, as for 30 years my family has participated in the annual Edgartown Sailing Regatta. Only reasons of health prevented my wife from accompanying me.

On Chappaquiddick Island off Martha's Vineyard, I attended on Friday evening, July 18th, a cookout I had encouraged and helped sponsor for a devoted group of Kennedy campaign secretaries. When I left the party around 11:15 p.m. I was accompanied by one of these girls, Miss Mary Jo Kopechne. Mary Jo was one of the most devoted members of the staff of Senator Robert Kennedy. She worked for him for four years and was broken up over his death. For this reason and because she was such a gentle, kind and idealistic person, all of us tried to help her feel that she still had a home with the Kennedy family.

There is no truth whatever to the widely circulated suspicions of immoral conduct that have been leveled at my behavior and hers regarding that evening. There has never been a private relationship between us of any kind. I know of nothing in Mary Jo's conduct on that or any other occasion—and the same is true of the other girls at that party—that would lend any substance to such ugly speculation about their character. Nor was I driving under the influence of liquor.

Little over a mile away the car that I was driving on an unlit road went off a narrow bridge which had no guard rails and was built on a left angle to the road. The car overturned into a deep pond and immediately filled with water. I remember thinking as the cold water rushed in around my head, that I was for certain drowning; then water entered my lungs and I actually felt a sensation of drowning; but somehow I struggled to the surface alive. I made

immediate and repeated efforts to save Mary Jo by
diving into the strong and murky current, but suc-
ceeded only in increasing my state of utter exhaustion and alarm.

My conduct and conversation during the next several hours, to the extent that I can remember them,
made no sense to me at all. Although my doctors
inform me that I suffered a cerebral concussion as
well as shock, I do not seek to escape responsibility
for my actions by placing the blame either on the
physical and emotional trauma brought on by the
accident, or on anyone else. I regard as indefensible
the fact that I did not report the accident to the
police immediately. Instead of looking directly for a
telephone after lying exhausted on the grass for an
undetermined time, I walked back to the cottage
where the party was being held, requested the help of
two friends, Joe Gargan and Paul Markham, and
directed them to return immediately to the scene with
me (it then being sometime after midnight) in order
to undertake a new effort to dive down and locate
Miss Kopechne. Their strenuous efforts, undertaken
at some risk to their own lives, also proved futile.

All kinds of scrambled thoughts—all of them confused, some of them irrational, many of which I
cannot recall, and some of which I would not have
seriously entertained under normal circumstances—
went through my mind during this period. They were
reflected in the various inexplicable, inconsistent and
inconclusive things I said and did—including such
questions as whether the girl might still be alive
somewhere out of that immediate area, whether
some awful curse actually did hang over all the
Kennedys, whether there was some justifiable reason
for me to doubt what had happened and to delay my

report and whether somehow the awful weight of this incredible incident might in some way pass from my shoulders. I was overcome, I am frank to say, by a jumble of emotions—grief, fear, doubt, exhaustion, panic, confusion and shock.

Instructing Gargan and Markham not to alarm Mary Jo's friends that night, I had them take me to the ferry crossing. The ferry having shut down for the night, I suddenly jumped into the water and impulsively swam across, nearly drowning once again in the effort, returning to my hotel around 2 a.m. and collapsed in my room. I remember going out at one point and saying something to the room clerk. In the morning with my mind somewhat more lucid, I made an effort to call a family legal adviser, Burke Marshall, from a public telephone on the Chappaquiddick side of the ferry, and then belatedly reported the accident to the Martha's Vineyard police.

Today, as mentioned, I felt morally obligated to plead guilty to the charge of leaving the scene of an accident. No words on my part can possibly express the terrible pain and suffering I feel over this tragic accident. This last week has been an agonizing one for me, and for the members of my family; and the grief we feel over the loss of a wonderful friend will remain with us the rest of our lives.

Kennedy put aside the prepared text. He folded his hands, looked directly into the camera and appeared to continue the speech extemporaneously. However, large cue cards, picking up the text of the speech were held up out of camera range by Joe Gargan:

These events and the publicity and innuendo and whispers which have surrounded them, and my admission of guilt this morning, raises the question in my mind of whether my standing among the people of my state has been so impaired that I should resign my seat in the United States Senate. If at any time the citizens of Massachusetts should lack confidence in their Senator's character or his ability, with or without justification, he could not, in my opinion, adequately perform his duties and should not continue in office.

The people of this state—the state which sent John Quincy Adams, Daniel Webster, Charles Sumner, Henry Cabot Lodge, and John F. Kennedy to the United States Senate—are entitled to representation in that body by men who inspire their utmost confidence. For this reason I would understand full well why some might think it right for me to resign.

This would be a difficult decision to make. It has been seven years since my first election to the Senate. You and I share many memories. Some of them have been glorious, some have been very sad. The opportunity to work with you and serve our state has been much of what has made my life worthwhile.

And so I ask you tonight, the people of Massachusetts, to think this through with me. In facing this decision, I seek your advice and opinion. In making it, I seek your prayers. For this is a decision that I will have finally to make on my own.

It has been written:

"A man does what he must—in spite of personal consequences, in spite of obstacles and dangers and pressures—and that is the basis of all human morality. And whatever may be the sacrifices he faces if he follows his conscience—the loss of his friends, his fortune, his contentment, even the esteem of his fellow men—each man must decide for himself the course he will follow. The stories of past courage cannot supply courage itself. For this each man must look into his own soul."

I pray that I can have the courage to make the right decision. Whatever is decided, whatever the future holds for me, I hope I shall be able to put this most recent tragedy behind me and make some future contribution to our state and mankind whether it be in public or private life. Thank you and good night.

9

WITH "HUCK" LOOK IDENTIFIED AS THE MOST DAMAGING witness at the inquest, Edward Hanify retained private investigator J.E. Gautreau of Confidential Services, Ltd., of Arlington, Massachusetts, to conduct an investigation of Look and other witnesses scheduled to testify.

Look was "a little bit upset" when he found out. "Investigators for Kennedy were knocking on doors all over Edgartown asking old ladies if I get drunk or run around with women. Well, everybody knows that I don't. But even if I did, that wouldn't change what I saw."

Gautreau's investigation was discontinued at Richard McCarron's request, "Because it didn't work. The press got on to him too fast, and so did people in Edgartown." Look's reputation was exemplary, McCarron said. "My attitude was, 'Why are we investigating 'Huck' if he's telling the truth?'" The fact an investigation had been undertaken was McCarron's only question about Look's story, he said. "I didn't have any doubt 'Huck' saw what he said he saw."

McCarron sought to resolve the mystery of that confrontation himself. Securing a registry list of property owners assessed at Chappaquiddick as of January 1, 1969, he questioned only a few residents seeking to locate a "black sedan" with an "L7" Massachusetts registration before giving up. "It was the same problem the investigator had," McCarron said. "People just got on too fast to what I was doing."

McCarron was deeply involved in an investigation of another kind, having received permission from George Killen for tests to be performed on the accident car impounded at state police barracks at Oak Bluffs. McCarron had asked the tests not be divulged, but Daniel I. Murphy, captain of the state police bureau, didn't want his agency accused of "favoritism" by allowing experiments to be conducted in secret. Murphy released the information that an investigation into the "physical factors" of the accident was being undertaken by a 10-man team from the Arthur D. Little Company, a research consultant firm of Cambridge.

Senator Kennedy was concerned about statements made by John Farrar that Mary Jo Kopechne could have breathed in a pocket of air long enough to have been rescued if help had been sought out immediately after the accident. "Above all, Kennedy has told friends, he wants to prove that Mary Jo could not have survived in the submerged car even if he had immediately summoned help, instead of waiting nine hours to report the accident," a delay which had provoked speculation "that Senator Kennedy had tried to avoid being implicated in any report of Miss Kopechne's death." The idea that Kennedy had bolted from the scene and abandoned Mary Jo Kopechne to die a slow, terrifying death by asphyxiation was so damaging to his case as to have prompted experiments to determine how long she could have survived after the accident.

A mannequin of her approximate size and weight was used in a test during which the accident car was flipped over and jarred with the same impact with which it had struck the water in Poucha Pond. The mannequin was thrown into the rear seat of the car with a force "sufficient to stun, and possibly disorient a human being."

Hoisted by a wrecker into a position to simulate that in which it was discovered, the car was filled with water from a state police garden hose to determine how quickly air had been displaced in the backseat. Two days of tests concluded that Mary Jo Kopechne had remained conscious for "one to four minutes." She could have been revived up to ten minutes after losing consciousness.

John Farrar regarded the tests as "worse than useless," he said. "How they can recreate the conditions, I don't know. Filling a car with water is not the same as having it submerged. It seems certain they are doing all this to try to discredit my evidence. But the big difference is, I went down to where a girl was trapped in a submerged car—the consulting firm didn't." In Farrar's opinion, there was no way to duplicate the circumstances of the accident short of sinking the automobile all over again.

Farrar's pronouncements about an air bubble having sustained Mary Jo Kopechne's life, and that she might have been saved if he'd been called at the time of the accident had brought him some highly critical mail, he said. "But I stand on my belief."

McCarron was not concerned about Farrar's testimony, he said. "John was a little screwy on the subject of the accident." A "summer kid" who'd moved to Edgartown in 1965, Farrar had held press conferences at the Turf 'n' Tackle to explain his theories about the accident. No matter how expert his testimony was, Farrar had, by pontificating at such length about the accident, literally talked himself out of any credibility as a witness.

But Arena, too, was skeptical about the value of tests conducted to replicate the accident. The accident car's wiring having been destroyed by vandals, a battery was placed directly on headlights to indicate the dimmer switch had been on high-beam at the time of the accident. Using a 1969 Chevrolet with the same headlight configuration as the accident car, a test of "visual factors" was conducted to reproduce what the human eye would see approaching Dike Bridge at night. Motion pictures revealed the bridge was visible "less than 3 seconds, if approached at 20 miles per hour." Still photographs taken under the same conditions showed at a distance in excess of 100 feet, headlights struck the ground in front and to the left of the bridge then were deflected upward, "Almost as though one's headlights had been turned out"—an abrupt change in light intensity that could well distract a driver. As the car reached the bridge, headlights came down to illuminate the rub rail, and the realization that the road over the bridge angled to the left.

Arena clocked the test car at 20 miles per hour for an experiment during which brakes were applied the instant front wheels touched the bridge. Although the automobile stopped in 31 feet and did not plunge over the side, the test indicated that, even allowing reasonable reaction time, "Braking only will not prevent a car traveling at a speed of 20 miles an hour from going over the rail," a result that appeared to confirm Registry Inspector

George Kennedy's report of his examination of skid marks on the bridge and "other conditions." Inspector Kennedy had calculated the car had been operated "at approximately 22 miles per hour" at the time of the accident, an assessment Arena discounted entirely. "Maybe an engineer could do it," he said. "But I seriously doubted 'Red' Kennedy would be able to tell much from the smudge marks I saw on the bridge."

As a state trooper, Arena knew skid marks were evaluated on the basis of tire depth and length of skid. Dike Road was dirt, sand and gravel. If Senator Kennedy had attempted to brake before the accident, no skid marks would show up on that surface. Markings on wood were difficult to measure and even harder to evaluate. In Arena's opinion, Senator Kennedy had not attempted to brake at all but had driven straight over the side of Dike Bridge. Without braking there could be no skid marks. And without skid marks, no way for "Red" Kennedy—or anybody else—to estimate rate of speed.

As part of the tests commissioned on behalf of Senator Kennedy a plan and elevation of Dike Road's approach to the bridge was prepared from direct survey and aerial photographs. A consulting engineer found existing conditions at Dike Bridge "well below the minimum standards set by commonly used engineering criteria." The absence of warning signs, guardrails, lights or reflectorized markers made the accident site particularly hazardous at night. Underwater photographs of the tide and current patterns in Poucha Pond and the location of the accident car were taken by a scuba diver.

Senator Kennedy's swim across the ferry channel was restaged by a person of his approximate weight and stature, preceded by "some alcoholic intake" to approximate conditions the night of the accident. Dukes

County Sheriff John Palmiera refused McCarron's request to administer a breathalyzer test, since "no criminal aspect" was involved in the experiment. Palmiera said, "We use the breathalyzer when someone is arrested. It isn't a toy."

Such elaborate and contrived experiments scandalized Edgartowners with rumors of thousands of dollars spent on, "The best evidence money can buy." In contrast to the sums at the disposal of Kennedy's defense team, a special appropriation bill passed by the legislature allowed the County of Dukes County to borrow $15,000 to pay for the scheduled inquest. In pursuit of justice, Edgartown couldn't compete with the Kennedy fortune.

With costs of the defense mounting up, McCarron requested compensation to cover day-to-day expenses. A check for $5,000 was issued from Park Plaza, Inc., the Kennedy family corporation. When McCarron complained he hadn't received the money, an investigation revealed the check had been stolen from a tampered mail chute in the Pan Am building in New York, and cashed the same day at a bank nearby.

But more than money, scientific and legal expertise was being thrown at the problem of Chappaquiddick. A tireless propaganda machine was seeking to disperse the cloud of scandal hanging over Senator Kennedy, described as "hurt and shaken" by rumors attaching to the episode. Kennedy was disturbed, in particular, by "one widely-accepted line of speculation that there was never any question of catching the ferry and that, after the accident, he at least entertained the notion of concealing his role by reporting that Miss Kopechne had been alone in the car."

To repair the damage done to his career as a political leader "willing to speak out on important issues," Kennedy used the occasion of a testimonial dinner in

Boston for the retiring president of the American Cancer Society to deliver a harsh condemnation of the Vietnam war as a conflict that was "eroding the health, the economy and the moral and spiritual strength" of the nation "as surely as any disease that attacked the body."

Response from a distinguished audience was "lukewarm at best," the speech described as "a palpable dud," and "a lackluster performance," that revealed Kennedy was still suffering under the shadow of unanswered questions about the death of Mary Jo Kopechne.

That the speech had not aroused marked enthusiasm was less surprising than, "Ted Kennedy had been audacious enough, less than two months after Chappaquiddick," to speak so indignantly about such virtues as moral strength, Sylvia Wright observed in *Life* magazine. Wright ascribed Kennedy's regained spirit to his job as Senate whip, "And acceptance of the fact that he must—and will—face further questioning about the accident." Forbidden by court order from making public statements about the case, Kennedy had come to realize, "There was much more he should have said immediately after the accident. The advice taken, the solutions worked out in those rainy days inside the Hyannis Port compound were not, he now feels—along with many friends and family advisers—the best advice and solutions." Thus, the forthcoming inquest was "less frightening to him than it is essential." Kennedy was eager to satisfy the widespread demand for information about the accident, Wright reported. "If necessary, he would probably be willing to be interviewed by newsmen on a TV panel."

Kennedy had tried to answer questions the Kopechnes had about their daughter's death, he said. "For the rest, it will all come out. The questions . . . all the answers. And I think people will understand. But it will just have to wait."

For the Senator's office to generate favorable stories, seeking to exculpate him of any blame in the accident and dismiss the dangers of the forthcoming inquest didn't sit very well with Edward Hanify, reflecting a continuing struggle between the Senator's lawyers and his political advisers. (Hanify had opposed the Senator making the TV speech, Dick McCarron said. "Everyone agreed it had been a mistake.")

Efforts to rescue the Senator's political reputation were jeopardizing the defense of his case. The peril of possible criminal charges issuing from the inquest was serious enough not to risk further damage to his legal position by indulging in a public dialogue about the accident. McCarron received a call from Hanify during a dull interval in the case. "Nothing much was going on," McCarron said. "Hanify felt there was just too much interference with Ted's political people in the management of the case; that we couldn't function properly as attorneys under those circumstances." Their insistence on issuing public relations statements was making a legal defense of Senator Kennedy virtually impossible. Hanify intended to resign from the case unless he was given free rein, without interference from Kennedy's staff or advisers. He was soliciting the support of other lawyers employed in the Senator's defense to present a united front. McCarron agreed to join Hanify, Judge Clark and his son, to walk off the case.

Hanify's ultimatum had its effect. McCarron said, "He stayed on; we all did." Kennedy could not bear the spectacle of his legal team abandoning his defense prior to the argument of his appeal before the Massachusetts Supreme Judicial Court.

Senator Kennedy would make no political appearances while court action was pending, his office announced. The "self-imposed moratorium" would prevent the Senator from participating in a special election in the 6th congressional district in Massachusetts. Kennedy had given his "implied endorsement" to Democratic candidate Michael Harrington before the accident, but since that time had no connection with the campaign. Because the election was regarded as a possible trend-setter for 1970, Edmund Muskie and George McGovern had appeared for the candidate. Hubert Humphrey and other prominent Democrats were scheduled to campaign. Kennedy wasn't going to take part, a Harrington aide said. "The decision was made not to invite him, because it wouldn't help."

But denying Senator Kennedy a public platform from which to discuss the accident didn't stanch the tireless efforts of his staff to defend the legal blockade imposed upon the inquest. Friend and political ally, Senator Birch Bayh, among others, took up the cudgel. Ted Kennedy was "anxious" to tell all he knew about the accident, Bayh said. "The matter has to be cleared up completely. I think Ted wants to make available all the information."

Bayh had been involved in an accident himself which had left him so confused he had assumed for 24 hours that he was responsible for someone's death. Not until he called the home of the deceased to extend his sympathy had he learned that another driver was to blame. Bayh cited the incident "as a possible explanation" for Senator Kennedy's failure to report the accident for more than nine hours. It was "too early to tell" how badly Chappaquiddick had hurt Kennedy's political career, Bayh said. "Some polls say he's completely through. My judgment is that this is not completely true. He has a tremendous hold on young people. It amounts to almost worship. And young people are prone to forgive and forget."

Bayh's analysis was not borne out by a survey published by *The Boston Globe* on September 22, revealing that the greatest drop in approval for Senator Kennedy in Massachusetts had occurred in 18- to 20-year olds. The slide was so precipitous that it fueled rumors of an impending resignation. Governor Francis Sargent went so far as to request a review of the procedure for naming Kennedy's replacement. Should the Court strike down his appeal and require Kennedy to testify at a public inquest he might resign before facing revelations of wrongdoing. That speculation appeared uppermost in Edward Hanify's mind when he rose to argue the appeal before the Massachusetts Supreme Judicial Court.

Hanify wanted the Court to determine whether the inquest statutes had become "outmoded" by recent U.S. Supreme Court decisions. Unless new ground rules were laid down, the procedure could be unconstitutional, Hanify said. The evil to be averted was the use of a judicial proceeding prior to a formal indictment, generating massive and gratuitous publicity which could prejudice Senator Kennedy's case, and deprive him of a fair trial in any subsequent criminal action. As evidence, Hanify brought a "compendium" of press clippings to the courtroom, and cited the Dr. Sam Sheppard murder case* as an example of publicity developing from a flood into a tidal wave."

Hanify asked the Court to bar the press and public from the inquest, disqualify Judge Boyle from presiding and, should the inquest reflect any wrongdoing on Senator Kennedy's part, to suppress the report and transcript of testimony until the conclusion of any prosecution or trial.

Assistant Attorney General Joseph Hurley hit the
publicity issue head-on. The prejudice complaint in
Sheppard, he argued, had occurred after the accused
was arrested and during the course of his trial. In
reversing the conviction, the Supreme Court had not
held reporters should be excluded from the courtroom,
but that the trial judge should have controlled them
better. The principle that justice could not survive
behind walls of silence had long been reflected in the
Anglo-American distrust of secret trials. A responsible
press was "the hand maiden of effective judicial administration," especially in criminal cases, not only publishing information about trials, "but guarding against
miscarriages of justice by subjecting police, prosecutors
and the judicial process to public scrutiny." The courts
had, traditionally, refused to place any limitation on
freedom of the press even while "sometimes deploring
its sensationalism." The news media was not concerned
with Senator Kennedy's guilt or innocence with regard
to the death of Mary Jo Kopechne, but his career as a
U.S. Senator and his future in national politics, Hurley
said. The inquest should be public for the same reason
Kennedy had gone on television, "To end innuendo and
gossip." The peak of publicity had been reached follow-

---

*On July 4, 1954, 31-year-old Marilyn Sheppard, wife of Dr. Sam Sheppard, a
wealthy osteopathic neurosurgeon, was beaten to death in her suburban Cleve-
land home. Sheppard was tried and convicted of second degree murder in one
of the most highly publicized and sensational trials of modern times. In
November 1961, a young lawyer, F. Lee Bailey, appealed the case, charging that
the press had "deliberately and with malice" published articles implicating
Sheppard. At the culmination of a series of appeals, on June 6, 1966, the U.S.
Supreme Court overturned Sheppard's conviction, citing "the trial judge's
failure to protect Sheppard sufficiently from the massive, pervasive, and prejudicial publicity that attended his prosecution." At a second trial six months later,
Dr. Sheppard was found not guilty.

ing the Senator's broadcast.

The rights of privacy of the other petitioners had been lost, Hurley went on, "By their action of attending a social event with Senator Kennedy, a person of great prominence." Their constitutional rights would be infringed only if publicity adversely influenced the outcome of a judicial proceeding to which they became parties. Publicity about an open inquest did not make the publicity prejudicial; a secret inquest would also generate publicity. "Because of the extreme interest in the case, you might close the doors, but you couldn't keep secret what was going on inside," Hurley said. Reporters would work diligently to discover what was going on and, as a result, inaccurate information about the proceedings would be published.

An inquest could clear a person of suspicion as well as indicate guilt, "And preserve the good name of Mary Jo Kopechne, even though she is not a party to the hearing," Hurley said. Nor was an inquest a first step on a stairway leading to criminal prosecution, but complete in and of itself, its purpose served when the presiding judge filed a report to the Superior Court. "There may be criminal proceedings," Hurley said. "But I know of none."

If Hurley and Hanify were unwilling to declare exactly what was feared in the holding of an inquest, Henry Monaghan did not hesitate to do so in a brief filed on behalf of the Civil Liberties Union of Massachusetts as *amicus curiae*. Unless criminal prosecution were commenced against Senator Kennedy or some other person, "It is doubtful there is any constitutionally-acceptable basis for holding an inquest." Under Boyle's ground rules, Kennedy could stand publicly accused of Mary Jo Kopechne's death. Having pleaded guilty to one offense arising out of the accident,

Kennedy could be reported to be the person "whose unlawful act or negligence appeared to have contributed thereto," Monaghan said. "Accordingly, he faces the possibility of a manslaughter proceeding."

If the district attorney desired a public trial, then Senator Kennedy must be afford the procedural safeguards which attended the criminal process, Monaghan argued. If the Commonwealth wasn't willing to grant those rights, it could proceed by way of a grand jury whose proceedings were always secret. While an indictment may be returned, "Senator Kennedy would be spared the intense glare of one-sided publicity," which could jeopardize his right to a fair trial.

10

DINIS DID IN FACT, GET HIS CHANCE TO GIVE THE CASE to the grand jury when it reconvened in Edgartown on October 14. As he had done so often before in this case, he went to the brink—and then shied away from taking the plunge. Juror Theresa Morse recalled that Dinis was "all fire and brimstone" when he addressed the jury. "He said he wanted our help, because he was going to 'get' Kennedy if it was the last act of his life; he wasn't going to buy his way out of this one. It didn't matter how much money he had, or how much power he had, the facts were going to be known."

The jury could help the most "by not getting in the way at all," Dinis said. The body of Mary Jo Kopechne was going to be exhumed, an autopsy performed, and an inquest held. Dinis was going to get to the truth of the matter and then, "If he needed us, he was going to call us back," Morse said. "The grand jury was all in a loving spirit of cooperation. And we cooperated with Mr. Dinis."

That the grand jury was recessed, instead of discharged, provoked speculation Dinis was leaving the door open to present the case to them should the Supreme Judicial Court rule his inquest request was invalid. A recess allowed time for the court to decide Kennedy's appeal.

But Dinis was either playing fast and loose with the grand jury or rehearsing in public a private ambivalence about prosecuting Ted Kennedy. He would not seek a grand jury investigation, regardless of the Court's decision, he said a week later in Wilkes-Barre. "Such an action would place me in control of the investigation and I prefer a judge to retain that responsiblity."

Dinis was about to have his day in court. A second Kopechne motion to dismiss the request for an autopsy had charged the amended petition had included no new evidence to indicate an autopsy would add anything to what was already known about Mary Jo Kopechne's death. Nor was an autopsy needed to solve a crime Dinis had reason to suspect had been committed.

"Our position is quite simple: No crime, no criminal conduct, no autopsy." Kopechne lawyer Joseph Flanagan said. "We are going to do everything we can to stop the district attorney from going on a fishing expedition. He can't seek his evidence in the grave without providing facts that the evidence is there."

Judge Brominski dismissed the motion. In his ruling, he said the "interests of the public" and the Kopechnes could best be served "by developing the facts at a hearing" that would allow the court to resolve the question of exhumation and autopsy without further delay. It was a decision so obvious, some legal observers wondered why it had taken Brominski three months to make it.

Before the hearing, Flanagan visited Edgartown to interview potential witnesses, examine the scene of the accident and ask Arena "only routine questions about my investigation."

Flanagan denied Senator Kennedy was involved in the fight against exhumation. "Ted Kennedy would very much like to have an autopsy performed," Kennedy spokesman William vanden Heuvel said. The Senator was "in close touch" with the Kopechnes, aides in his office revealed. "His battle against a belated autopsy was less than for legal reasons—his advisers think it could only help him—than in sympathy with their opposition." Flanagan refused to say whether "the Kopechnes are paying for this trip or is someone else?"

The Kopechnes had turned down "a few offers" of help with the legal expenses of barring the autopsy. "This is our responsibility," Joseph Kopechne said. "We haven't stopped to think about the cost of it all. We'll worry about that when it's all over. The lawyers have been very good, letting us pay what we could afford. Even if we're overruled, it won't be the end of it. We'll go as high as we have to."

George Killen was also in Edgartown lining up witnesses for the hearing. His most delicate mission was to persuade Dr. Donald Mills to testify on behalf of the petition. Killen wasn't blaming anybody but himself for releasing the body of Mary Jo Kopechne without autopsy. He had no intention of corroborating Dinis' claim to have ordered an autopsy on the morning her body left Edgartown.

Kopechne lawyers had already expressed an interest in having him testify, Mills said. It was debatable which side Mills would benefit the most.

There was no question whose side John Farrar was on when Killen took his detailed statement. As captain of the search and rescue division of Edgartown's volunteer fire department, Farrar had made his own study of the accident. In Farrar's version, the car had been travelling 30 miles per hour and had hit the water at a 45-degree angle. Kennedy had been able to escape, "Because with the roll of the car, the driver's side window would have been the last one submerged," Farrar said. Mary Jo Kopechne had assumed "a conscious position" in the backseat. "She was rebreathing her own air. The oxygen content was lowering from 21% as she used it up and replaced it with carbon dioxide," Farrar said. "As the CO_2 builds up, you breathe heavier and heavier; the emotional trauma is extensive. Try putting a plastic bag over your head and breathing. You can feel the anxiety coming over you. Then try to imagine that bag being held over your head by a 300-pound wrestler, and think of having to struggle to get out of that situation knowing you might be breathing your last. It's a very, very scary situation. The anxiety that sets in is just unbelievable."

The length of time a pocket of air remained in a submerged automobile was a matter "no human being can swear to, but she could have lived for a good while after the car went off the bridge." Farrar estimated, "She was alive, easily an hour."

Farrar produced a sketch of the body's position in the accident car redrawn three times by an artist, "To become as close as possible to that which I observed," to aid in the presentation of his testimony at the exhumation hearing.

Impressed by the passionate advocacy with which Farrar expressed his theories, Killen thought, "He's going to make one helluva witness."

So did Assistant District Attorney Armand Fernandes who accompanied Killen to take Farrar's statement which, if allowed to become part of the record could be very damaging to Ted Kennedy.

Thanks to a special $15,000 appropriation voted by the Massachusetts legislature to fund the investigation, Dinis was able to assemble a panel of 14 witnesses and experts to appear with him in Wilkes-Barre.

It was 10 a.m. on October 20, 1969, when Judge Brominski opened the hearing in Luzerne County courthouse. While welcoming reporters to the packed courtroom, Brominski also admonished them to observe certain rules for this case. "You will be required to remain in your assigned places until such time as Court recesses or adjourns a session," he said. If reporters left the courtroom, they would not be readmitted until the following day. Any violation of his guidelines would result "in the revocation of your press pass."

But no reporter was likely to chance missing out on the first courtroom confrontation in the case—a virtual preview of the postponed inquest.

Armand Fernandes, who had prepared the hearings case, opened argument by reciting the Massachusetts law granting district attorneys authority to request autopsies on their own authority. As his first witness, Fernandes called Police Chief Dominick Arena to the stand to relate the events of Saturday, July 19, after he had been summoned to Dike Bridge on Chappaquiddick and returned to Edgartown police station to receive a statement about the accident from Senator Kennedy.

Representing the Kopechnes, Joseph Flanagan objected to the Senator's statement being placed into evidence as "hearsay."

Fernandes was not concerned "with establishing what

the Senator said at this time was true—*that* may be hearsay." The report was being offered "as a statement made of the facts and circumstances," he said. "We're not concerned with the truth of it."

Brominski refused to allow it. To rule an official police document inadmissible in a judicial proceeding stirred reporters in the courtroom to murmurs of disbelief—no matter which legal hairs were being split.

Dinis himself examined the next witness, scuba diver John Farrar. Battered by news media accusations that he was "prejudiced, biased and anti-Kennedy," Farrar had retained attorney Herb Abrams for advice and assistance in the preparation of his testimony. Farrar had anticipated being asked for "a professional opinion" as to whether Mary Jo Kopechne could have been alive upon her removal from the submerged car if sufficient air had been trapped. It was a chance he would not get. Brominski dismissed as "immaterial and irrelevant" the statement Abrams made to introduce Farrar's testimony.

Dinis did not ask Farrar about airlocks, or Mary Jo Kopechne's longevity underwater, restricting him to a description of the automobile's position in Poucha Pond, the damage sustained to it in the accident, and the process whereby Farrar had recovered the body.

If Farrar's potentially damaging testimony could be eluded, "Huck" Look's couldn't be. His very appearance on the witness stand—robust and ruddy, a plainspoken rustic—was a rebuff to those who had questioned his credibility. Look's description of a car whose driver appeared "confused," and his recognition of the same automobile the next morning when it was dragged from Poucha Pond was devastating in its direct and simply stated sincerity. Under oath, Look placed the time of his encounter at "approximately 12:40 a.m.

to 12:45 a.m., Saturday morning," a direct challenge to Senator Kennedy's version of the accident.

There wasn't much Flanagan could do but try to cast doubt on Look's ability to read a license plate in the dark. But Look easily disposed of that cavil. "There were lights on the car—back-up lights, tail-lights and number plate lights."

"Did it appear to you that the driver of the car was in a confused state?" Flanagan asked.

"Yes, sir," Look said.

"Yet, despite the fact that this driver appeared to be in a confused state, you did not follow the car or make any attempt to stop it that night, did you?"

"No, sir," Look said.

"Did the car move away from you slowly?" Flanagan continued.

"No sir," Look answered. "I would say, hurriedly." Before he could call out an offer of help, the car had driven off at "approximately 25 to 30 miles per hour," Look said. "There was a lot of dust. All I could see was just the lights going down the road."

Look's appearance on the witness stand brought Herbert "Jack" Miller to the courtroom to confirm Bernie Flynn's intelligence about him as the most dangerous witness expected to testify at the inquest with regard to the time of the accident and the reason for Kennedy's wrong turn to avoid confrontation with a police officer.

Informed by two reporters during a recess that Miller was attending his examination of Look, Fernandes recognized his name "as a Washington attorney of some ability, like you would know F. Lee Bailey, by his reputation," he said. "But there was no association with anybody, as far as I was concerned."

If Look represented the most danger to Kennedy's case at the inquest, Dr. Donald Mills was the biggest obstacle Dinis had to get over in order to secure an exhumation and autopsy.

Dinis left his examination to Fernandes.

Mills was sticking to his diagnosis. His examination of Mary Jo Kopechne had revealed, "She had the characteristic foam that goes with a drowning case. She had no evidence of injuries . . ."

Flanagan drove the point home forcefully under cross-examination.

"In your examination of the body, Doctor, did you find any signs of foul play?"

"I did not," Mills said.

"Did you have any reason to believe there was any criminal conduct that may have resulted in the girl's death?"

"I have no reason to believe any such thing!" Mills snapped.

But Dinis had a corps of experts waiting in the wings to dismember Mills' testimony and to call into question the soundness of his drowning conclusion.

Among them was Dr. Cyril Wecht, coroner of Allegheny County, Pennsylvania. External examination alone frequently failed to reveal if body organs had been lacerated, several kinds of poisonings, a fractured skull or a broken neck, Dr. Wecht testified. It was possible for a competent forensic pathologist to perform an autopsy on an embalmed body buried four months and still arrive at "quite substantial and valid opinions with more than a reasonable degree of medical certainty" that could verify, modify or even completely negate Dr. Mills' findings.

That Mary Jo Kopechne had been found inside an automobile suggested the possibility that a significant injury may have occurred prior to her death. Dr. Joseph Spellmen, medical examiner for the city of Philadelphia, testified. He found "little significance" in the pink froth about the nose and mouth of the victim, a phenomenon which appeared in other forms of death such as heart failure and drug overdose.

"Would this include manual strangulation?" Fernandes asked.

Flanagan objected to the question. So did Brominski. He wanted Fernandes, "To stay away from that line of questioning."

The question came up, "Because we were trying to find out what other kinds of injuries could result in the things the medical examiner found in Mary Jo Kopechne's case," Fernandes said, later. Dr. George Katsas, who performed most autopsies on Cape Cod, had alerted the district attorney that strangulation was one of several things that could have brought about the same conditions. "That," Fernandes would say later, "was why the question was used."

A highly respected forensic pathologist, formerly attached to the department of legal medicine at Harvard Medical School, Katsas would have performed an autopsy on Mary Jo Kopechne had Dinis ordered one.

On the witness stand, Katsas testified that an experienced forensic pathologist could recognize and evaluate aspects of disease and injury in an embalmed and exhumed body. In Katsas' opinion, external examination alone "did not exclude the presence of internal injuries, fractures or ruptures of organs which may have contributed to the death or even have caused the death."

Preparing Katsas to appear at the hearing, Killen had some questions of his own not put to him on the witness stand. Prudish and puritanical, disliking "smutty talk," Killen had, nevertheless, considered Bernie Flynn's opinion that a sexual interlude could have accounted for the hour and a half between the time Ted Kennedy said he'd left the cottage and the time "Huck" Look saw the car at the intersection. Lab tests for semen had been "negative," but Mary Jo Kopechne had not been wearing underpants, Flynn pointed out. "So obviously you couldn't make a test on underpants. Any seepage would be on the slacks."

Katsas had performed the difficult post-mortems in the Costa murders. Microscopic examination of vaginal smears taken from two badly mutilated bodies buried for six weeks in a Truro woods had revealed the presence of male spermatozoa. Killen wanted to know if it was possible to detect evidence of sexual intercourse in an embalmed body buried for over three months.

Finding sperm was "remote" in exhumed bodies, Katsas told Killen, but no one could be absolutely certain without an autopsy, and serological tests of a vaginal swab for "semen markers"—a number of common chemicals found in male ejaculate, a biological fluid rich in certain proteins. Semen contained 400 times more of the enzyme acid phosphatase than any other body fluid. An "AP-positive swab" would indicate "maybe" on sexual intercourse.

If sperm were not detected, the serologist looked for "sperming"—a chemical contained in seminal states—and P-30, a protein found only in semen. Sperm and P-30 were the only "conclusive tests." But, Katsas added, chances of finding either were slight. In Killen's judgment, the odds were so long that there was no point in raising these issues while Katsas was on the stand.

Now on the offensive, Flanagan called Dr. Werner Spitz, deputy chief medical examiner for the State of Maryland, who testified that it was "good as impossible" for a pathologist to determine whether a person had drowned or asphyxiated. "You may exhume the girl and examine her and still not know whether she drowned," Spitz said. Drowning was one of the most difficult diagnoses to make in forensic pathology because it so frequently resembled other causes of death.

How then, Dinis wanted to know, could Spitz be "so medically certain" Mary Jo Kopechne had drowned?

"Because of the circumstances which are being related to me," Spitz said. "The question here is: 'Shall the deceased be exhumed?'"

"That is *not* the question!" Dinis snapped. "The question is whether or not you can eliminate any other cause of death other than drowning."

"She may have injuries which I cannot determine upon external examination of the body and . . ."

That was good enough for Dinis. "No further questions," he said, cutting Spitz off.

"I didn't finish the sentence!" Spitz protested.

Brominski allowed Spitz to continue, and may have wished he hadn't.

"She may have injuries," Spitz went on. "There is no question in my mind that at this point she also inhaled water. It is also apparent to me from the record that she lived for a certain time underwater. Otherwise, why should the froth have developed? You're talking about pink foam," Spitz added, warming up to his subject. "That foam is the combination of water and protein that is being shaken. And the shaking action is the breathing action. So she breathed, that girl. She *breathed!* She wasn't dead instantaneously. You're not going to find a cause of instantaneous death whether you exhume her or you don't."

Flanagan looked stricken. In his peroration, Spitz had medically corroborated John Farrar's long-held opinion—heretofore excluded from testimony—that

Mary Jo Kopechne had lived for a time in the submerged car, an admission that, because it came from a "defense" witness, was especially damaging.

Flanagan got Spitz off the witness stand in a hurry, but the damage was done. Not only had Spitz legitimatized Farrar's theories, he had floated a pretty good reason to exhume and autopsy Mary Jo Kopechne himself.

"The issue Kennedy's lawyers feared the most was the *Welansky* decision as a basis for bringing a manslaughter charge," Fernandes said, later. "They were scared to death of that case, because an omission to act constitutes negligence under the law." If Senator Kennedy had abandoned a living, breathing passenger in his car and his failure to notify police and rescue personnel could be shown to have contributed to her death, he was guilty of manslaughter.

Flanagan moved swiftly to recoup. He called Spitz' boss, toxicologist Dr. Henry Freimuth. Chief medical examiner for the State of Maryland, Freimuth testified that the stains on the blouse Mary Jo Kopechne had worn at the time of her death were "typical" of those produced by the pinkish froth discharged from the nose and mouth of drowning victims. "In a drowning case there will be blood foam in the airway from the rupture of very fine, little vessels. You don't need much blood to give it a pinkish hue," Freimuth said. The foam could come out of the mouth, roll down the side of the face and stain the clothing of a drowning victim, stains "that gave positive benzidine reactions." In a few, incisive phrases, Freimuth had disposed of Dinis' blood evidence.

From having heard the testimony in the courtroom, Joseph Kopechne felt more than ever, "We do not want an autopsy. My wife and I are unalterably opposed to it.

It would be just like another funeral for us. We feel that they had a chance at an autopsy, it wasn't performed, and we absolutely do not want it now. We see no value in it at all."

Brominski adjourned the session at 9:00 p.m. Dinis was "very near completion." Asked if he planned to call Senator Kennedy as a witness, Dinis said, "That's always a problem, but not as of tonight."

It certainly would be a problem. Having cancelled a speech in August to be available in case his presence were required at an inquest, Kennedy was now out of the country, attending a NATO meeting in Brussels. Inevitably, speculation arose that Kennedy's lawyers did not want him testifying in open court, particularly when Dinis intended to present evidence of "inconsistency" between the Senator's two public statements about the accident.

Dinis took the witness stand the next day to defend himself against charges of inaction in the case and his failure to have called for an autopsy earlier. There was no provision of law which put Dinis under an obligation to make an immediate investigation of any case in his jurisdiction, he said. It was customary for district attorneys to take charge of cases, "When the investigation by local authorities was either unsatisfactory or incomplete." Dinis would not have ordered an autopsy, "Unless I was informed of sufficient facts to give me a reason to." After that information had been made available to him, Dinis had "positively ordered" an autopsy, only to be told, "The body had already been flown off the island by the Kennedy people." As chief law enforcement officer for the Southern District, Dinis was "not satisfied" with the cause of Mary Jo Kopechne's death as determined by Dr. Mills.

Brominski ordered Dinis' comment stricken from the

record. It made no difference whether Dinis was a district attorney, a judge, or a defense counsel, he said. "You cannot come to a conclusion unsubstantiated by facts."

Dinis was undaunted. An autopsy, he said, was necessary to ascertain the legal cause of death and to resolve the contradictions between Senator Kennedy's two statements about the accident. Dinis had wanted the statements entered into evidence in lieu of the Senator's presence as a witness in the courtroom.

But with Kennedy's accident report excluded there was no point in offering Kennedy's television speech as Dinis proceeded to do. Without the police report, there would be no basis for finding "inconsistency."

Once again Flanagan objected. The speech was "a self-serving declaration," immaterial and irrelevant to the issue of the hearing. Inexplicably, Brominski said he would allow it—if an accurate reproduction could be found. Dinis had a transcription of the broadcast supplied by radio station WBZ in Boston.

So it was that, into the packed courtroom, came the voice of Teddy Kennedy, delivering a speech that sounded to many just as facile and manipulative as it had originally, and every bit as "indefensible" as Kennedy said his actions after the accident had been.

Brominski adjourned the hearing at 3:15 p.m. An hour later, he was handing out refreshments and dancing with supporters at a campaign rally. Brominski bristled at the suggestion he intended to delay his decision to exhume and autopsy Mary Jo Kopechne until after the election. "That's unfair! I have to wait until the court stenographer completes the transcript of the hearing before I can make a ruling."

Dinis told reporters as he left the courthouse that he was satisfied that the allegations in his amended petition

had been proved. "I can't think of a single instance
where we were disheartened. Everything we tried to
achieve was achieved." Dinis had been "treated fairly,"
he said. "We will abide by the decision. I don't think
we'll go any further on appeal if we lose."

11

ON TUESDAY, NOVEMBER 18, 1969, AT 11:04 A.M., JOSEPH P.
Kennedy died in his sleep at the age of 81. A White
House Mass was celebrated at St. Francis Xavier church
in Hyannis by Richard Cardinal Cushing. Senator
Kennedy paid tribute to Ann Gargan's "loyalty, devo-
tion and great love" as companion to his father, invali-
dated by a stroke in 1961.

In lieu of a eulogy, Kennedy read a passage from a
privately printed volume of family reminiscences, *The
Fruitful Bough,* written by Robert Kennedy whose 44th
birthday the funeral also observed. Three days later, a
memorial Mass at the church marked the sixth anniversary of John Kennedy's assassination.

Senator Kennedy objected to "certain unjustified
statements" in *Newsweek's* obituary of his father, com-
plaining, "We who are in public life must learn to live
with petty gossip and baseless slander." Senate col-
leagues were reported "astounded" by Kennedy's resil-
ience, his determination to reassert strong leadership on
major issues. Kennedy was "regaining confidence and
spirit," recovering remarkably from the gloom of Chappaquiddick. "Great spells of depression had been com-
monplace then for what he had done to the family
name and the memory of his slain brothers." Among

friends, Kennedy was again able to laugh and enjoy himself. Those who knew Kennedy said, "He's snapping back."

The Senator acknowledged he was feeling better. Not having to read about the case in the newspapers every day helped. He was now awaiting the inquest, "eager to clear up all the remaining questions" about the accident; and stepping-up his schedule of public appearances on behalf of his campaign for re-election. Kennedy denied he would seek to surpass his record 1.2 million winning margin in 1964, he said, "But I think we'll win big."

Crimmins was back chauffeuring Kennedy in Boston. Gargan was once again advancing campaign stops. It was politics as usual, and a public display of confidence. With an informer installed in the district attorney's office, Kennedy was assured of a pipeline to whatever disclosure might come out of further police investigation. But the inquest cast shadows nonetheless over an election it was conceded Kennedy had too formidable a lead to lose.

But the Senator had every reason to be optimistic. He had altered a judicial procedure which had stood for 82 years, stilled as much talk about the case as it was possible for his media controllers to do, and blocked a police investigation while at the same time maintaining a public posture of "cooperating fully" with the inquiry. His attorneys had won every legal round in the courts. Another victory was imminent.

On Wednesday, December 1, Judge Brominski barred the exhumation of Mary Jo Kopechne. There was, he ruled "No evidence" to indicate "anything other than drowning had caused the death of Mary Jo Kopechne." Even if an autopsy revealed a broken neck, a fractured skull or the rupture of internal organs,

"None of these would be incompatible with the manner which this accident occurred," Brominski said. Evidence of blood stains on Mary Jo Kopechne's clothes had been "wholly consistent with death by drowning."

To justify his ruling required that Brominski travel peculiar corridors of logic. That the accident may have occurred at 12:50 a.m. on July 19, rather than 11:15 p.m. on July 18 did not suggest a cause of death other than drowning. While an acknowledgment of "Huck" Look's testimony, Brominski dismissed the idea that even if Senator Kennedy had lied about the time of the accident and his reason for turning onto Dike Road, this was not sufficient to cast doubts on other reported aspects of the accident. To consider any other cause of death at this time, "would give loose rein to speculation unsupported by any medical facts of record," Brominski said. In fact, the lack of an autopsy guaranteed speculation and rumor would continue to flourish.

Brominski had taken the opposition of the Kopechnes into account in making his decision, he said. While their disapproval was no absolute bar to an autopsy, "In view of the facts presented, their objections are well taken." In so holding, Brominski challenged a ruling by the Pennsylvania Supreme Court in 1956 which said that the purpose of an inquest was to protect the public. Any doubts about a death favored holding an autopsy. If a coroner failed to do so, "It is the duty of the Court to have the body exhumed and an autopsy performed." Yet, by finding Mary Jo Kopechne could have died from no other cause than drowning, and that an autopsy was not necessary to establish legal cause of death, Brominski had established his own judicial precedent.

The decision came as no surprise to Dinis. As a candidate in a heavily Democratic district, Brominski had played politics every step of the way, holding the petition hostage to his own re-election bid. He even waited until he won a new ten-year term on the bench before making his ruling.

To criminal attorney Melvin Belli, "The irony is, the public's impression that the JFK autopsy was unsatisfactory, and now Teddy Kennedy's female companion gets none," he said. "The Kennedy family is hiding the actions of those two days. They've gone around parading themselves as sponsors of the little people and yet let that little person in the back seat of a car go unexamined to the grave."

Brominski's ruling pleased Gwen Kopechne. "I can't tell you how wonderful I feel," she said. "Now, I know my daughter will not be disturbed and will be at rest. I could never have gone up to that cemetery again, if I knew she'd been disturbed." She and her husband had agreed, "If in any way we had felt we were obstructing justice by fighting exhumation of Mary Jo's body, we would have yielded in favor of an autopsy. But I know what drowning is; I've seen drowned persons before. When I saw my daughter, I could tell she had drowned."

But speculation of sexual misconduct attached to the accident was clearly on Mrs. Kopechne's mind, anxious as she was to preserve her daughter's reputation against reports challenging the characterization of Mary Jo as the most straight-laced of the Boiler Room crew. One such report said that at a party in Washington one month before Chappaquiddick, Mary Jo was "somewhat vocal and demonstrative, even sitting on the lap of a man who was someone else's date. She had a little too much to drink and was flirting and more girlish than usual."

Mrs. Kopechne said, "Mary Jo was a wonderful girl, so aware and full of life. Nobody had announced it—

how could you? But there was an examination of my girl. And it showed she was a maiden lady."

Now the Kopechnes were "patiently waiting" for the start of the inquest. That Judge Boyle had refused to allow them or their attorneys to attend was upsetting, "Because we're the parents of this girl and it's as if we don't exist," Mrs. Kopechne said. "The whole thing has been a mystery." Joseph Kopechne added, "There's a lot of questions we want answered. You have to have a daughter to know how we feel. People are saying: 'Your kid was dead before she hit the water.' But I don't give a damn about the public. I just want to know what happened."

Senator Kennedy telephoned the Kopechnes to express his pleasure at Brominski's ruling, "because I realize how much it means to the Kopechne family. It increases their peace of mind and I'm grateful for that." It was now Kennedy's hope, "that the authorities in Massachusetts will move forward so the entire matter can be concluded as soon as possible."

12

PROMPTLY AT 9:00 A.M., CLERK OF THE COURT TOMMY TELLER formally opened the inquest *re: Mary Jo Kopechne.* The inquest was not a prosecution of anyone, Judge Boyle told all lawyers and witnesses he'd summoned to the courtroom in order to explain the purpose of the inquest, the results it was intended to accomplish and the rules of procedure under which it would be held. The courthouse did not provide facilities for the sequestering of witnesses. However, he made it clear, "Wit-

nesses after testimony, are ordered not to discuss their
testimony with anyone except his or her counsel."

Boyle recognized a difficulty in this regard with Red-
mond and Daley representing a substantial number of
witnesses. "I don't want any attorney who heard what
one witness said in the courtroom to reveal to another
witness what the testifying witness said," Boyle said. He
was specifically ordering attorneys, "Not to discuss the
testimony of one client with another client."

Hanify wanted to be sure he understood Boyle's
order, "As an implicit instruction to all counsel present
that we are to respect the privacy of the proceedings,
and are not to discuss with the press what goes on."

But if Hanify and the other lawyers knew perfectly
well what Boyle had in mind, that would not prevent
Boyle's instructions from being repeatedly and deliberately violated.

Boyle excused everyone from the courtroom except
Dinis and his legal staff. In keeping with the secrecy
order imposed by the Supreme Court, state police
trooper Robert Enos and George Killen were asked to
leave. Killen joined Bernie Flynn, assigned security
duty in the corridor outside the courtroom, to summon witnesses. Before the inquest in September was
postponed, Dinis had proposed Chief Arena and other
Edgartown locals testify first, followed by those who
had attended the party at Chappaquiddick—with the
exception of Paul Markham, Joseph Gargan and Senator Kennedy. Dinis had wanted them questioned last,
and in that order. Judge Boyle, however, had in mind a
different arrangement. He would not "Keep a U.S.
Senator waiting."

Dinis now proposed Robert Malloy, general account-
ing supervisor of the New England Telephone Company, to lead off the inquest. Boyle suggested Malloy

not be called until some foundation was made to indicate his testimony was relevant.*

Dinis called Senator Edward Kennedy as the inquests
first witness. Kennedy entered the courtroom accompanied by Hanify and Clark. He took the witness stand in
the near-empty courtroom to put on the record what he
had avoided direct questioning about for more than five
months. Because Kennedy had waited so long, "Anything he says will be weighed against two earlier statements that were less than persuasive," *The New York
Times* said. "There is a risk that even the most dignified
and straight-forward mea culpa could bring his public
career to a humiliating end."

But there was nothing straightforward about what
Kennedy put on the record. It was, instead a lattice-
work of evasions and omissions, of half-truths and
obfuscation patched together by a phalanx of lawyers
and advisers.

Arriving at Edgartown on Friday, July 18, Kennedy
was brought to Chappaquiddick and driven over Dike
Bridge as a passenger in a 4-door Oldsmobile 88 operated by Jack Crimmins. After a swim at East Beach,

---

* Malloy's attorney Charles Parrot came to the courtroom prepared to offer four
lists of telephone calls charged to Kennedy credit card accounts in Boston,
Washington and Virginia and those billed to Park Agency, Inc., of New York—
none of which showed any calls made during the hours after the accident or
before Kennedy called Helga Wagner after 8 a.m. at the Shiretown Inn.

In a nine-page memorandum for his own files, Parrot observed, "There was
no discussion about records of calls by putting dimes and quarters in the box,
collect calls, or charging calls to your home number." Parrot denied any
telephone company records had been withheld.

Fernandes said, "Judge Boyle was only interested in a list of calls made from
Martha's Vineyard on July 18-19 as relevant to the issue of whether the Senator
had telephoned anyone after the accident." Compiled in chronological time-
sequence, the record, "Doesn't at the moment tell me anything," Boyle said,
when Malloy was on the witness stand. Dinis saw "no harm" in offering the list
into evidence.

Kennedy was returned to Edgartown for the Regatta race, then checked into the Shiretown Inn, "visited with friends," and returned to Chappaquiddick to soak his back in a hot tub until party guests arrived in a rented Valiant around 8:30 p.m.

Kennedy had initially tended bar, "Then, I think, most of the individuals made their drinks after that." He had "engaged in conversation and recollections" with guests "which were old friends of myself and our families." He left the party at "approximately 11:15 p.m.," Kennedy testified. "I was talking with Miss Kopechne perhaps for some minutes before that period of time. I noticed the time, desired to leave and return to the Shiretown Inn and indicated to her that I was leaving and returning to town. She indicated to me that she was desirous of leaving, if I would be kind enough to drop her back at her hotel. I said, 'Well, I'm leaving immediately,' spoke to Mr. Crimmins, requested the keys for the car and left at that time." While his chauffeur drove him on practically every occasion, "Mr. Crimmins, as well as some of the other fellows attending the cookout were concluding their meal, enjoying the fellowship and it didn't appear to me necessary to require him to bring me back to Edgartown," Kennedy said, slipping easily into euphemism to provide the first obfuscation in his testimony. (Drunk, truculent, demanding everyone leave, Crimmins could hardly be said to be "enjoying the fellowship."*)

Although the question wasn't asked, Kennedy denied "any personal relationship whatsoever with Mary Jo Kopechne." He had never been out with her when "we were not in a general assemblage of friends, associates or members of our family." He left the party for the ferry landing, travelled down "I believe it is Main

Street," and taken a right turn on Dike Road.

Kennedy disposed of "Huck" Look's anticipated testimony in short order: At no time had he driven into Cemetery Road, backed the car up or seen anyone between the cottage and Dike Road, he said. "I did not stop the car at any time. I passed no other vehicle. I saw no other person."

Kennedy was driving "approximately twenty miles an hour," taking "no particular notice" that Dike Road was unpaved, or that he was not heading for the ferry landing. He had applied brakes, "A fraction of a second before he was on the bridge and about to go off," he said. "The next thing I recall is the movement of Mary Jo next to me, the struggling, perhaps hitting or kicking me. And I, at this time, opened my eyes and realized I was upside-down, that water was crashing in on me, that it was pitch black. And I was able to get a half gulp, I would say, of air before I became completely immersed in the water. I realized that Mary Jo and I had to get out of the car."

Kennedy tried to get the door open by "reaching what I thought was down, which was really up," and feeling alongside the door panel to see if the window was open. "And I can remember the last sensation of being completely out of air and inhaling what must

---

* Crimmins testified he didn't know why he hadn't driven the Senator to the ferry. The Senator had called him out of the cottage to the front yard. "He told me that he was tired and that he wanted to go home and go to sleep. He told me he was going to take Miss Kopechne back, that she wasn't feeling well; she was bothered by the sun on the beach that day." Kennedy asked for the keys to the car." It was his automobile and I gave them to him. I didn't question him." Crimmins was sure Kennedy left a 11:15 p.m., "Because I looked at my watch."

The District Attorney's office had information that Crimmins didn't want to give Kennedy the keys to the car and offered to drive him to the ferry landing. Armand Fernandes revealed after the inquest, "But like other investigations we did, it was nothing conclusive."

have been a half a lung-full of water and assuming that
I was going to drown. And the full realization that no
one was going to be looking for us until the next
morning, that I wasn't going to get out of that car alive;
then, somehow, coming up to the last energy of just
pushing, pressing, and coming up to the surface," he
said. "I have no idea in the world how I got out of
that car."

Judge Boyle asked Kennedy to describe what he had
seen as he was driving along Dike Road, "From the
point when you first saw the bridge."

"I would estimate that time to be fractions of a
second from the time that I first saw the bridge and was
on the bridge," Kennedy replied.

"Your attention was not diverted by anything else?"
Boyle said.

"No, it wasn't," Kennedy said.

"I want to go into the question of alcoholic bever-
ages," Boyle said.

Kennedy had "two rum and cokes at the party,"
he said.

Boyle wanted "to go back before that," he said. "I
think you said you visited friends at the Shiretown?"

Kennedy had "a third of a beer at that time." But
Boyle hadn't gone back far enough. Kennedy didn't
mention the victory party on Ross Richards' boat after
the Regatta race at which he'd drunk three rum
and cokes.

After Boyle was assured that Kennedy had been
made aware of his constitutional rights with regard to
self-incrimination, he said, "Were you at any time that
evening under the influence of alcohol?"

"Absolutely *not*," Kennedy said. He had been "absolutely sober" when he drove over the side of Dike
Bridge, the scene of the accident Dinis was anxious to

resume his questions about.

After Kennedy escaped from the submerged automobile, he was swept away "by the tide that was flowing at an extraordinary rate" in Poucha Pond. Wading up to his waist, he started back to the car, "gasping and belching and coughing," to commence diving in an attempt to rescue Mary Jo Kopechne. Prevented from doing so by the fast current, he'd returned again and again to try to gain entrance to the car, "until at the very end, when I couldn't hold my breath any longer."

"You were fully aware at the time what was transpiring?" Dinis said, leading up to the question of "shock" after the accident.

Kennedy knew what was coming and tried to slide under the question. "Well, I was fully aware that I was doing everything that I possibly could to get the girl out of the car. And that my head was throbbing and my neck was aching and I was breathless and, at that time, hopelessly exhausted." Kennedy was careful not to say "in shock" as Dinis was inviting him to.

"But there was no *confusion* in your mind about the fact that there was a person in the car?" Dinis asked, a direct reference to Kennedy's television speech.

Kennedy ducked the question again. "I was doing the very best I could to get her out," he said. On the last of seven or eight attempts to get into the car, he realized, "I just couldn't hold my breath any longer. I didn't have the strength to come down even close to the window or the door. I knew that I just could not get under water any more." He had lost contact with the car, let himself float to shore, "And I sort of crawled and staggered up some place and was very exhausted and spent on the grass."

Kennedy rested on the bank for 15 to 20 minutes. After he regained his breath, "I started going down that road walking, trotting, jogging, stumbling as fast as I possibly could. It was extremely dark and I could make out no forms or shapes or figures. The only way that I could see the path of the road was looking down the silhouettes of the trees of the two sides." To his knowledge, "I never saw a cottage with a light on," he said, artfully—not to say lights were lit. The walk back to the cottage had taken "approximately 15 minutes." A white Valiant was parked 15 to 20 feet outside the front door. "As I came up to the back of the vehicle, I saw Ray LaRosa and I said, 'Ray, get me Joe.'" Kennedy climbed into the back seat of the car. Gargan came out; then, Paul Markham. Kennedy told them, "There's been a terrible accident. Let's go," and returned to Dike Bridge. "I believe that I looked at the Valiant's clock and believe that it was 12:20 a.m.," Kennedy said, contriving to establish the time of the accident. (When it was discovered by *The Boston Globe* in 1974 that the Valiant rented for the regatta weekend had no clock, Kennedy admitted, "I made a mistake about a clock being in the Valiant that wasn't there." Caught in the lie, he sought to correct his answer retroactively. "I am also aware that Paul Markham had a watch on and that I did determine the time.")

Kennedy had not participated in the rescue efforts undertaken by Gargan and Markham, he said. "But I could see exactly what was happening and made some suggestions."

"You were fully aware of what was transpiring at that time?" Dinis reiterated, giving Kennedy another chance to lay claim to the "shock" of his police report and the "scrambled thoughts" of his television speech.

Kennedy wouldn't do it. He was "fully aware" that Gargan and Markham "were trying to get in that car and rescue that girl."

But Dinis was now leading up to another, inevitable subject: "Was there any effort made to call for assistance?"

There was no way around this question. It had to be answered. Kennedy said, "No, other than the assistance of Mr. Gargan and Mr. Markham."

"But they *failed* in their efforts to recover Miss Kopechne . . . " Dinis said.

At this critical point in the examination, Judge Boyle interrupted to ask Kennedy to leave the witness stand and the courtroom.

Boyle told Dinis that, in his view, the purpose of the inquest was to determine whether criminal conduct had contributed to the death of Mary Jo Kopechne, and not whether poor judgment or duplicity may have followed.

Armand Fernandes recalled "quite a tussle with Boyle about all questions stopping after the car hit the water and Mary Jo died. He wanted only testimony relating to whether the Senator or anyone else had acted criminally in her death—not what anybody did afterward." To Fernandes a defendant's behavior *after* a crime was material to any inquiry, especially in view of the omission to act liability under the *Welansky* decision for manslaughter.

Vigorously protesting the limitations Boyle was seeking to place on his examination of witnesses, Dinis threatened to walk out of the inquest unless he was allowed more latitude to ask questions. Faced with the disruption of the inquest and the possible collapse of the entire enterprise, Boyle reluctantly acceded. But he would continue to cut Dinis off in the middle of questions to admonish him, "I want to avoid as much as possible any trial technique." Boyle did not suggest what other method there was to elicit information from a witness. Both were in the dark about inquest procedures. Neither Dinis nor Boyle had ever participated in one before.

"Was there any particular reason why you did not call either the police or the fire department?" Dinis said when Kennedy resumed the witness stand twenty minutes later. Kennedy tried to duck the question. "Well, I intended to call for assistance and report the accident to police within a few short moments after going back into the car."

Neither Boyle nor Dinis had any objection.

"Did something transpire to prevent this?" Dinis said.

Now at the most critical point in his testimony, Kennedy's answer on the record would be scrutinized, pondered and tested for years to come. Kennedy didn't want to undergo interrogation. He said, "If the Court would permit me, I would like to be able to relate to the Court the immediate period following the time that Mr. Gargan, Markham and I got back in the car."

Neither Boyle nor Dinis had any objection.

"I believe it was about 45 minutes after Gargan and Markham dove and they likewise became exhausted and no further diving efforts appeared to be of any avail. And they so indicated to me and I agreed," Kennedy said. "So they came out of the water and came back into the car and said to me, at different times as we drove down the road towards the ferry, that it was necessary to report this accident.

"A lot of different thoughts came into my mind at this time about how I was going to really be able to call Mrs. Kopechne at some time in the middle of the night to tell her that her daughter was drowned, to be able to call my own mother and my own father, my wife," Kennedy said, evading the issue of notifying the police and rescue personnel. "Even though I knew that Mary

Jo Kopechne was dead and believed firmly that she was in the back of that car, I willed that she remained alive. I was almost looking out the windows trying to see her walking down that road." Gargan and Markham understood this feeling, but said it was necessary all the same to report the accident. "And about this time we came to the ferry crossing and I got out of the car and we talked there just a few minutes," Kennedy continued. "I just wondered how all of this could possibly have happened. I also had sort of a thought and the wish and desire and the hope that suddenly this whole accident would disappear. I related this to Gargan and Markham and they reiterated that this had to be reported, and I understood at the time . . . that it had to be reported. And I had full intention of reporting it. And I mentioned to Gargan and Markham something like, 'You take care of the girls; I will take care of the accident!'—that is what I said and I dove into the water."

Kennedy had been prompted to give instructions "not to alarm Mary Jo's friends that night," and conceal the accident from the others at the party, "Because I felt strongly that if these girls were notified that an accident had taken place and Mary Jo had, in fact, drowned, that it would only be a matter of seconds before all of those girls, who were long and dear friends of Mary Jo's, would go to the scene of the accident and enter the water with, I felt, a good chance that some serious mishap might have occurred to any one of them."

With that admonition, Kennedy dove into the channel. As he started to swim into the tide, "I felt an extraordinary shove, the water almost pulling me down. And suddenly I realized that I was in a weakened condition, although as I had looked over that distance between the ferry slip and the other side, it seemed to me an inconsequential swim. But the water got colder, the tide began to draw me out. And for the second time that evening I knew I was going to drown," Kennedy said. "I remember being swept down toward the direction of the Edgartown Light and well out into the darkness. And I tried to swim at a slower pace, to be able to regain whatever kind of strength that was left in me. And some time after that, I think it was about the middle of the channel, the tide was much calmer, gentler." Reaching the other shore he pulled himself onto a beach. He said, "And all the nightmares and all the tragedy and all the loss of Mary Jo's death was right before me again."

Kennedy found his way to a parking lot adjacent to the Shiretown Inn "almost having no further strength to continue, and leaning against a tree for a length of time, trying to really gather some kind of idea as to what happened." He went to his room, took off his clothes and collapsed on the bed. He was conscious of a throbbing headache, pains in his neck and back strain, "But what I was even more conscious of was the tragedy and loss of a very devoted friend," Kennedy added. Hearing noises "around me, on top of me, almost in the room," Kennedy put on dry clothes and opened the door to his room. "I saw what I believed to be a tourist or someone standing under the light off the balcony and asked what time it was. He mentioned to me it was, I think, 2:30, and I went back into the room," he said, and betrayed the guile and calculation of his prepared testimony. In his television speech, Kennedy had specifically identified "a room clerk." Russell Peachey had corroborated the conversation the next day. Now, in the lawyer-reworked version, it was more prudent not to be so exact following his traumatic swim, as to appear to suggest a motive in seeking a witness to his presence far from the accident scene. Kennedy also neglected to say

he had descended the stairs to provoke the encounter; or
that the "tourist" had asked if he required "any further
assistance.

Dinis did not ask why Kennedy had not availed
himself of this opportunity to report the accident. By
his rambling discourse, Kennedy had avoided explaining why authorities had not been notified of the accident or help sought to retrieve the body of Mary Jo
Kopechne from his submerged car.

"I never really went to bed that night," Kennedy
continued. "Even as that night went on and as I almost
tossed and turned and walked around that room . . . I
had not given up hope all night long that, by some
miracle, Mary Jo would have escaped from the car."

Kennedy had spoken to the desk clerk the next morning, then to Ross Richards and Stan Moore. (He had
been about to conduct these conversations without
betraying any sign of distress about the accident,
Kennedy explained in 1976 to *The Boston Globe*,
"Because I was still in the frame of mind of false hope,
that perhaps with the dawning of a new day, all the
nightmare events of the evening before would have been
washed away." But all hope "absolutely disappeared,"
when Gargan and Markham arrived at the Shiretown
Inn, Kennedy said. "From just the look on the faces I
could tell that as hard as I had prayed for her survival,
that Mary Jo was dead. Up to that time I really tried to
will her existence and her life.")

"They asked had I reported the accident and why I
hadn't reported the accident," Kennedy said on the
witness stand. "I told them about my own thoughts and
feelings as I swam across that channel . . . that somehow when they arrived in the morning that they were
going to say that Mary Jo was still alive. I told them
how I somehow believed that when the sun came up and

it was a new morning that what had happened the night before would not have happened and did not happen.

13

MARY JO KOPECHNE WAS NOT THE ONLY CASUALTY OF that "tragic accident." To some, Chappaquiddick had a decisive impact on the Nixon presidency, too. First, there was, in the Nixon White House, euphoria at the prospect of not having to face Kennedy for re-election. But that euphoria had hardened into an atmosphere of spite and vendetta, Dan Rather observed in *The Palace Guard.* "It may be said that Chappaquiddick helped unleash the forces that in time would make a wreckage of Richard Nixon's presidency."

It also made a wreckage of Kennedy's presidential hopes. His second chance at the White House since Chappaquiddick was swamped in the wake of Watergate. Citing "family responsibilities," Kennedy announced on September 23, 1974, his "firm, final and unconditional" decision not to seek the presidency in 1976. Kennedy denied Chappaquiddick was what drove him from running. He said, "I can live with my testimony."

The trouble was, few others could. Had Kennedy sought the nomination, "His most obvious problem is Chappaquiddick and the still unexplained discrepancies between his story and what seems to be indisputable facts," *McCall's* observed in November 1974. Chappaquiddick would have neutralized Watergate as a Democratic attack weapon. The lingering doubts about the accident had threatened a bitter, nasty, mud-slinging campaign. Already battle lines were being drawn. Bumper stickers had appeared to proclaim: Nobody Drowned at Watergate.

In anticipation of a Kennedy candidacy in 1976, *The Boston Globe* had undertaken an ambitious reinvestigation of the accident over the summer of 1974. "We are not out to drive Ted Kennedy from office," editor Tom Winship explained. "We are trying to get more details on an important story affecting a public figure who will continue to be important."

Senator Kennedy granted a two-hour interview to a team of investigative reporters to discuss the accident for the first time since the inquest. He continued to insist his version of the accident was accurate. The widespread skepticism about his inquest testimony was "unwarranted and unjustified," he said. "I attempted during the course of the inquest to respond to these questions completely, candidly, honestly and to the best of my ability." His conduct had been "irrational and indefensible and inexcusable and inexplicable," he said. "I was, at that time, obsessed by grief at the loss of a life. It was strictly a state of mind." But Kennedy cleared up none of the contradictions involved in the accident of "the nearly 100 discrepancies in the testimony and statements by several key inquest witnesses." Preferential treatment by law enforcement and judicial officials had saved Kennedy from being charged with serious crimes, including manslaughter, *The Globe* concluded in its four-part series. Routine investigative and judicial procedures had been either altered or botched numerous times by apprehensive officials in overwhelming deference to Kennedy's power and prestige. "Justice was not served, hard questions were not asked of witnesses and complaints and indictments not pursued."

Kennedy protested *The Globe*'s use of unnamed

sources to give prominence to charges that were "ugly, untrue, and grossly unfair," he said. "It is regrettable in the atmosphere of doubt and suspicion which enshrouds us as a people that the truth cannot compete with the unnamed source, the groundless suggestion and speculation which is nurtured by articles of sensationalism."

The facts, as Kennedy related them, "Are harsh, complete and cold on their own and no alteration of them to satisfy new suspicions could relieve me from the remorse and regret of which they constantly remind me." Kennedy attributed renewed interest in the accident to "a post-Watergate mentality," rather than any questions about the accident. "The problem is, they haven't been answered the way the writers would like to have them answered," he said. "The real story has been told. They're not going to find other kinds of facts, because they just don't exist."

The unanswered questions about Chappaquiddick had left Gwen Kopechne angry and frustrated. "Sometimes I'd like to scream a lot, but I'm trying to hold it back," she said. "It would be nice if somebody would speak up." Senator Kennedy had called her about *The Globe* articles. "He was worried that I might read some of it and become upset."

The Kopechnes came to Edgartown in June 1975, to seek answers to the case for themselves. Crossing on the ferry to Chappaquiddick, Gwen Kopechne pointed out the public telephone in the ferryhouse at the landing. Joseph Kopechne said, "I was rather afraid what her reaction would be when we went up to Dike Bridge. In fact, she reminded me of what part of the bridge the car went over—I had clean forgotten."

Among those they tracked down was "Huck" Look. Resigned to having his story questioned, Look said, "It just becomes, as I told everybody, a thing of credibility. If you want to believe him, fine. If you want to believe me, I've got nothing to gain in any way, shape, or form." (Evidently, Edgartown believed Look. They'd elected him sheriff.)

Look would "never live long enough" to believe he hadn't seen Ted Kennedy's car going down Dike Road an hour and a half after the Senator said the car went off Dike Bridge. "He's so sure of what he saw that it makes me think better about what really might have happened," Joseph Kopechne said. "It looks to me like there's a lot of unanswered questions now that I look at it objectively. The Senator gave me the story. I believed it, it's possible," Mrs. Kopechne said. "But at the same time I didn't have any questions to ask him. I was only listening to anybody that was saying anything to me. Now, I think I would give a little argument. Now, I'd have something to say."

The Kopechnes hesitated before entering the Turf 'n' Tackle shop to talk to John Farrar. "After all the inconsistencies and evasions," Farrar was "more convinced than ever the truth had not come out." Mary Jo Kopechne could have been saved if rescue personnel and equipment had been immediately called to the accident scene, he said. "I know she suffocated when her oxygen ran out. She didn't drown."

"I felt that boy is experienced enough so that he can make those statements. He convinced me real good," Mrs. Kopechne told Gerald Kelley, a local free-lance journalist. She added: "No matter how you look at it, it was an accident. What hurts me deep is to think that my daughter had to be left there all night. This is why we hold so bitter a feeling towards Markham and Gargan . . . I think Kennedy made his statement when he was still confused. In the state he was in, I do believe he couldn't think clearly. I think he was taking all this bad advice, and it just continued for days. He got so deeply involved in it, he couldn't back out and tell the truth. How is he going to change his story and get out of it? Now, he's in worse trouble than he would have been if he had come out and given the story himself, without anybody advising him."

Mrs. Kopechne wanted to talk to someone who had attended the party at Chappaquiddick. "I'd like to know what went on, what they were doing, what led up to Mary Jo leaving, and what happened afterward," she said. "I'm still waiting for something to happen. If you wait long enough you get what you're waiting for. That one day, I'll know everything I want to know. I don't want to hurt anybody. I think even the Senator has got enough problems."

The Kopechnes stayed at the Katama Shores motel where their daughter had been lodged during the regatta weekend. The bathroom wallpaper had fish floating through clouds of seaweed, Mrs. Kopechne said. Her daughter's death was with her "every time I entered that bathroom last night. It is with me every time I take a bath."

Chappaquiddick continued to hurt the Senator politically, but it did not affect his re-election to the Senate in 1976. A request for security personnel made through the State Police got Bernie Flynn assigned as Senator Kennedy's bodyguard for a campaign fund-raising party at Padanaram, a suburb of New Bedford. Told to mingle inconspicuously with guests, Flynn engaged Jack Crimmins in conversation and disclosed he'd been an investigator for the district attorney's office on the Chappaquiddick case. "I'm the guy that helped the Senator out," Flynn said. "I'm the one that told Stephen Smith about inquest evidence."

Flynn observed Crimmins in conversation with Senator Kennedy a short time later. "He was standing like ten feet away. I just happened to turn around at the right moment to catch Crimmins whispering in his ear. Kennedy was looking right at me with this startled look on his face, so I guess Crimmins told him who I was."

After the political affair, Kennedy invited Flynn to a private steak and lobster dinner in Plymouth hosted by Jack Campbell, a long-time supporter and owner of radio station WPLM. Campbell memorialized the occasion by taking photographs. Flynn wanted to have his picture taken with the Senator. Kennedy was happy to oblige his Chappaquiddick benefactor.

Kennedy won re-election, but the beneficiary of Watergate was Jimmy Carter. Outraged that a restoration should have been usurped by a political upstart from Georgia, Kennedy supporters revived rumors of a possible candidacy in 1980.

Returning to Edgartown again in 1978, the Kopechnes threatened to go on national television and "ruin Kennedy" if he tried to run for president. But by 1979, they had changed their mind. They still "didn't know the full story of the accident, but saw no reason to bring everything up again. Gwen Kopechne said, "Everyone makes mistakes. If he runs, we won't interfere."

Kennedy telephoned the Kopechnes to express regret for another avalanche of publicity as the tenth anniversary of Chappaquiddick approached. In fact, much of the publicity could have been avoided had Kennedy himself not granted numerous interviews, motivated by a desire to put the issue to rest before the campaign. Kennedy was not inviting reporters to ask him any questions they wanted about Chappaquiddick, "Because I will answer them, as I have answered them in the past."

The answers "seemed almost memorized," *The Washington Post* complained. An interview with the Senator about Chappaquiddick was "a distinctly unenlightening exercise, frequently punctuated by denials before the questions are complete. Sometimes Kennedy tries to fob off questions by alluding to what he said at the inquest. Occasionally he has to be reminded that he was never asked the question."

On the eve of the tenth anniversary of the accident, the Senator called the long-promised press conference to answer questions about the accident the inquest had left unanswered. "Many of the actions that I was involved in on that night were irresponsible," Kennedy said. But he did not believe Chappaquiddick posed the kind of tests he had met for 17 years in the Senate and would face as president. Kennedy had confronted issues of war and peace in public life since the accident, "And I felt no hesitancy about involving myself in them, and taking stands on many of them."

Kennedy hadn't been asked "a new question" about Chappaquiddick in ten years, he said. "There hasn't been a new fact that has questioned the position that I stated at the time of the tragedy and there cannot be." No information would ever challenge his sworn testimony, "Because it doesn't exist."

Chief Arena shared that view. In the ten years since the accident, "No one has ever found anything to support more than what I initially charged him with."

Still, one question continued to intrigue Arena: What had gone on from the time of the accident and Kennedy's report the next morning? "Expanding on it might lead to something that is beneficial to him, or it might not," he said. Arena wasn't sure he could vote for Kennedy if he ran for president. "I certainly couldn't wipe Chappaquiddick out of my mind." If Kennedy was a candidate, an investigation should be reopened and every facet of the accident reexamined, Arena said. "I still think the whole case deserves scrutiny."

Senator Kennedy had "cooperated fully and completely" with all of the law enforcement agencies involved, his press secretary replied, "What does Chief Arena want to be done?"

But Arena's doubts about a presidential candidacy were shared by others. "I don't think anybody can forget Chappaquiddick," Republican Congresswoman Millicent Fenwick told *McCall's*. Asked if there was any other issue besides Chappaquiddick that would defeat Senator Kennedy if he ran for president, Republican candidate Ronald Reagan replied, "Well, you mentioned one pretty good one."

Historian and former White House adviser Arthur Schlesinger, Jr., doubted Chappaquiddick would be a decisive factor in a presidential campaign. Ever since the accident Kennedy had been trying to redeem himself for those hours of panic. "He has become ever more serious, more senatorial, more devoted to the public good," Schlesinger said. "I think this ceaseless effort at self-redemption may be for Teddy Kennedy what polio was for FDR."

By June 1979, Kennedy was leading President Carter better than 2 to 1 in public opinion polls. Twice as many Democrats had "unfavorable" ratings for the President as for Ted Kennedy. All signs were pointing to Kennedy "positioning" himself for the run.

But Kennedy was adamant: He was not running, he said. "As I've said many times, I expect the President to be renominated. And I expect to support him.

Carter dismissed opinion polls as an accurate gauge of presidential popularity. "We've had some crises where it required a steady hand, a careful and deliberate decision to be made," he said. "I don't think I panicked in the crises,"—an observation regarded as a "coded reference" to the Senator's failure to report his accident for ten hours.

Kennedy did not expect Carter to bring up Chappaquiddick in the election, should he decide to seek the nomination, he said. "I think the President wants to talk about issues that are important to the country."

But the Senator got a foretaste of what he could expect as a presidential candidate at a political rally in Louisville, confronted by placards bearing Mary Jo Kopechne's name, and the effigy of a female corpse. In the face of continued questions about Chappaquiddick, Kennedy said, "People may not believe me or accept some of my answers, but the idea that the people who were there that night are holding back some secret is just all wrong." Repeated efforts by *The New York Times* to persuade Kennedy's friends to discuss the period after the accident were fruitless. "They refused, as they have for ten years to clarify the sequence of events on a night still cloaked in mystery."

Kennedy denied forbidding anyone to talk to the press. "Some have chosen to engage in interviews and conversations, others have not," he said. "I left that completely up to their discretion." However, Kennedy still had "a lawyer-client relationship with those who had given him legal advice after the accident." He did not want Joe Gargan or Paul Markham talking to reporters. On "Meet the Press," he continued to insist, "There is not going to be any new information that is going to challenge my testimony." If there was, "There would be absolutely no reason that I should consider remaining in public office, let alone run for the Presidency of the United States."

Chappaquiddick had not figured at all in Kennedy's

decision to seek the nomination, Stephen Smith reported. "The only major negative as always, was the assassination fear. But the judgment of everyone in the end was that you can't let that rule your life forever." Kennedy had made known, "His family was ready—if he was."

14

BUT KENNEDY WAS APPARENTLY NOT SO READY AS HE thought. On September 29, 1979, Roger Mudd of CBS News arrived in Hyannis Port to conduct an interview. Mudd tossed out a question he expected the Senator to hit out of the ball park: "Do you think, Senator, that anybody really will ever fully believe your explanation of Chappaquiddick?"

Kennedy struck out. He had found his behavior "beyond belief" himself, he said. Aired as part of a one-hour documentary special, Mudd devoted half the broadcast to the accident, asked Kennedy about other women in his life and characterized his marriage as "existing only on select occasions."

In an atmosphere of euphoria and great expectations, Kennedy formally announced his candidacy on November 7 at Faneuil Hall. But the promise of that candidacy, heralded since 1968, proved to be more seductive than the candidacy itself. Kennedy's campaign disintegrated a month later. Chappaquiddick was partly responsible for the dramatic plunge in Kennedy's popularity in opinion polls. "Doubts about the propriety of Kennedy's behavior at Chappaquiddick have risen significantly" in the six months since polls the previous

spring showed most Americans "willing to forgive and
forget" the incident.

Kennedy was having trouble attracting support from
politically active women. Feminist Betty Friedan "still
felt queasy" about Chappaquiddick, she said.

By the following January, Kennedy's advisers were
preoccupied with the impact Chappaquiddick was having on the campaign. The issue had been seriously
misjudged. Kennedy had allowed himself to be misled
by pollsters, friends and advisers into believing Chappaquiddick had faded as a potential source of trouble.
Campaign manager Stephen Smith called a press conference to refute a *Washington Star* report questioning
Kennedy's claim to have "nearly drowned" swimming
the channel after the accident. Hitherto undiscovered
evidence relating to tides and topography placed a cru-
cial element of his story in doubt. Aerial photographs
taken on May 15, 1969, had revealed the Katama open-
ing had sealed off, making Chappaquiddick not an
island separate from Edgartown. A rising tide no longer
flowed out of the harbor but in a reverse direction from
that which Kennedy described in his inquest testimony.

To challenge the story, Smith brought two admiralty
lawyers and an ocean engineer to the press conference,
the same team of experts that accompanied Kennedy to
a second conference the next day. Kennedy characterized the articles as "inaccurate, irresponsible and
incomplete," and charged the newspaper had misrepre-
sented what it had been told by tidal experts.

Edgartown Harbormaster Robert Morgan specu-
lated, "The tide that night could not have been other
than what Mr. Kennedy testified." Morgan had taken a
sailboat under tow to a pier close to the ferry landing
shortly before midnight on July 18, he said. "The tide
was low and quite slack, not moving in either direc-

tion," a condition that meant within the next 30 minutes to an hour, the tide would be running strongly out of the harbor.

The integrity of the entire Edgartown community was being seriously questioned by a barrage of national press stories about the accident, *The Vineyard Gazette* complained. When *The New York Times* questioned editorially whether Senator Kennedy had used "his enormous influence to protect himself and his career by leading a coverup of misconduct," readers would be led to believe investigative and prosecution officials on Martha's Vineyard had been negligent, inept or "subjected to influence," *The Gazette* observed. "The clearly-documented facts are that the tragedy was investigated by honest, competent police officers before it became known Kennedy was the driver of the car, and no basis was found for a complaint of speeding or reckless driving." The conduct of the entire case by Judge Boyle was "legally precise and impartial. One will go far in legal annals to find an abler judicial exercise."

Denouncing an article in *Reader's Digest* as "a very serious misrepresentation" of the operation of the automobile before the accident, Stephen Smith pointed out Senator Kennedy's rate of speed had been "officially accepted" by a Registry of Motor Vehicles investigation.

An accident analyst hired by the *Digest* to recreate conditions by computer revealed Kennedy had been driving on the wrong side of Dike Road, going approximately 34 miles per hour at the time of the accident. Kennedy had slammed on the brakes when he saw the bridge, skidded 17 feet along the road, another 25 feet up the bridge, and jumped the rub rail. Despite his braking effort the car had been travelling between 20 to

22 miles an hour when it hurtled 35 feet over Poucha Pond. That the Registry of Motor Vehicles had refused to release to the *Digest* a copy of its report of the accident "without written notarized authorization from Senator Kennedy himself," came as a surprise to Ronald Andrews, a private investigator specializing in laws pertaining to public records. He said, "I knew that according to Massachusetts law, anyone was able to gain access to the report." Andrews' request for a copy of the report was refused, because the document was protected "under The Fair Information Practices Act." (Registry counsel Rico Matera explained later, "The invasion of personal privacy in many instances outweighs the public's right to know, for the pertinent facts in this case have been spewed out to the public by the news media for many, many years.") Andrews appealed to the supervisor of public records of the department of the Secretary of State. Registrar McLaughlin was informed that a fatal accident report was not exempt from disclosure exceptions and directed him to provide Andrews a copy of the report.

Most interested to discover that Senator Kennedy's license had been thought for a time to have expired, Andrews turned the report over to Ralph Gordon, a veteran court reporter for the Springfield newspapers bureau in Greenfield, Massachusetts.

Gordon started checking out the story. Registry Inspector John Mellino told him, "I never liked all this cover-up stuff going on." Mellino dismissed the idea a license renewal could be left in the Tab Room for five months. Inspector Herb Burr couldn't explain the delay either, he said. "I have nothing to say about that."

Gordon was surprised to receive a call from Registrar McLaughlin himself. "I understand you've been talking to some of my men about Chappaquiddick," he said. McLaughlin had the Chappaquiddick file in front of him, he said. The Registry was the only agency "that went straight down the line on the case." Kennedy's license had been revoked on July 20, 1969, and surrendered to him personally by his lawyer, Judge Robert Clark.

Asked to explain the five-month delay in Kennedy's renewal card being replaced in the Registry's files, McLaughlin grew impatient. "You're insinuating something that doesn't exist and ascribing it to the 11-year-old memory of an inexperienced man working in the radio room." When Gordon emphasized he was reading from Inspector George Kennedy's report, McLaughlin hung up. His office was "not accepting any calls from you," Gordon was told when he tried to reach the Registrar again.

Gordon wrote the story and sent it to Springfield. "Beyond that, I didn't hear a thing, until I realized they weren't going to print it," Gordon recalled. "I finally called to ask why. They didn't question the story. The response was: 'Well, we just thought there had been enough on Chappaquiddick.' They were supporting Kennedy and decided, as a political thing, not to use it."

But Kennedy's campaign was haunted by Chappaquiddick. Spectators in Chicago spit on the candidate and called him "killer" as he went down State Street in a parade. A retired doctor carried a sign: "Do You Want the Coward of Chappaquiddick for President?" outside a senior citizen center Kennedy visited. Kara Kennedy, the Senator's 19-year-old daughter was told, "Your father killed a young girl about your age." "Negative feelings toward Kennedy are growing each month," *The Washington Post* reported in March. Nearly half the Democrats nationwide had "unfavorable views" of him, reversing polls conducted in November. The issue of the campaign had devolved upon the central mystery of Chappaquiddick and the death of Mary Jo Kopechne. "Last year, Kennedy decided he could be invulnerable even to this. He was wrong. Voters have not forgiven that he got away with it in 1969 and thought he could get away with it again in 1980."

Bernie Flynn—the man who bent the rules to aid Kennedy at the inquest had also had a change of heart about the Senator. "When Kennedy ran against Carter and he was screeching and yelling, I said to myself: 'Christ! This man doesn't deserve to be President.' I lost a lot of esteem for him."

Flynn had had no contact with the Senator since his security duty in 1976, and none whatever with Stephen Smith or Herbert Miller since their meeting at Logan airport a week before the inquest. Flynn had not found it necessary to cash in his job insurance policy. "If I was ambitious and they were deciding on two different occasions to make U.S. Marshals—I would have called up Stephen Smith to say, 'Now it's your turn to do me a favor,'" he said. "But it didn't cross my mind to see how far Kennedy would reciprocate." After 32 years in law enforcement, Flynn had had enough. He retired from the state police in 1980.

Stricken with cancer, George Killen had retired in 1975. Two months before his death in 1979, Killen was still lamenting Chappaquiddick as "the biggest mistake I ever made as a police officer." With the benefit of hindsight, Killen had dispensed with alternative theories and improbable scenarios to conclude Senator Kennedy had been drunk, in flight from "Huck" Look to avoid arrest and probably speeding at the time of the accident—his recklessness responsible for the death of Mary Jo Kopechne.

Chappaquiddick was equally fatal to Kennedy's presi-

dential aspirations in 1980. The Senator made a spectac-
ular appearance at the Democratic national convention
on August 12 in a moment of defeat unprecedented for
his family, to declare, "The dream shall never die." But
his campaign had been a long struggle to overcome the
stigma of Chappaquiddick. "The Senator told interviewer after interviewer that there was nothing new to
say about the accident. Neither the public nor the press
was persuaded," *The New York Times* said.

In his pursuit of the presidential nomination,
Kennedy had run against Chappaquiddick. And Chappaquiddick had won.

So decisive a defeat was regarded merely as a
"rehearsal" for 1984 by some of Kennedy's supporters.
Conventional political wisdom held that Kennedy
would not again have to face the specter of the accident.
"A personal issue that's a problem in one campaign
doesn't come back in the next," ran the argument.

By July 1982, polls were reporting Kennedy the leading candidate for the presidential nomination in 1984.
Seeking Senate re-election in Massachusetts against a
millionaire business man, Ray Shamie, hardly necessi-
tated the expenditure of $2.5 million—three times what
Kennedy had spent in 1976. Kennedy hoped to use the
1982 election as a "laboratory" to test ways to defuse
the Chappaquiddick issue that had disabled his 1980
presidential campaign, "So this is partly a test run for
the 1984 presidential sweepstakes," *The Wall Street
Journal* predicted, "and to salvage some of the fabled
political pride of the Kennedys."

But door-to-door polling revealed the "character
issue" a bigger factor than in 1976. Kennedy launched a
television advertising campaign created by a California
media consultant which concentrated on his
"compassionate side."

He needed just such image-burnishing: A 40-page comic book sent to two million Massachusetts households by Citizens Organized to Replace Kennedy portrayed him as a chubby black sheep, and zeroed in on his history of cheating at Harvard, Virginia traffic violations and Chappaquiddick. Kennedy's press secretary denounced the publication as, "The lowest level of propaganda. I find it appalling and hateful."

"The funny thing about it was, it's all true," Gargan said. Working on the campaign as usual, Gargan was taken to task "for sitting on your ass all winter doing nothing," by Ted Kennedy. Having joined Alcoholics Anonymous, involved in a courageous struggle to put his life back together, Gargan exploded. "I've given you 30 years of my life and what do I have to show for it? I'm a fool in the eyes of my own children because of Chappaquiddick. And that's *your* problem, not mine." One day, Gargan wanted the "real story" of the accident to be told.

Gargan stormed out of the campaign and resisted all overtures to return. A fixture for years as advance man, Gargan's absence was too conspicuous not to be accounted for. Kennedy's office explained the Senator's "gradual *drift* from close friends such as cousin Joe Gargan with whom he has clashed on the sensitive issue of abortion."

Despite the huge expenditure of campaign money, Kennedy ran less well than in 1976. The outlook for a presidential candidacy was not as promising as his advisers hoped. Exit polls of the 1.2 million who voted for him indicated over half wouldn't support him for president. If Kennedy believed "some kind of a magical TV spot" could neutralize Chappaquiddick and the kind of sustained barrage about it he would face in another presidential campaign he was mistaken. Polls conducted in New Hampshire, exposed to the "character ads" on Boston television, indicated they had failed to reduce the hostility felt by a large number of voters. The idea that Chappaquiddick would fade over time had not proven to be true. Kennedy was in the strongest position of any candidate to gain the 1984 nomination, "But given the negative feelings about him, he would be pursuing a smaller pool of voters." He could win, "But it would be another long season of personal harangues and lurid press for him." One adviser suggested outgrowing Chappaquiddick by 1988 and the years beyond, when voters might treat a man in his late 50s "more kindly for the indiscretions of his 30s."

Citing family responsibilities and his decision to divorce his wife, Kennedy announced he wouldn't be a candidate or accept a draft for the nomination in 1984. He didn't rule out a future presidential campaign. "I don't think it's any mystery that I would like to be President," he said. Kennedy denied he had withdrawn because of public doubts about his character stemming mostly from Chappaquiddick. But an aide confirmed the Senator had feared "the impact on his children of another round of accusations and inquiries about his role in the death of Mary Jo Kopechne."

For the first time in twenty-four years, a Kennedy was not a figure to be reckoned with at a Democratic national convention. Disappointed not to have been chosen as keynote speaker, Kennedy made a "gasbag of a speech," and appeared "incapable of seriousness" on the rostrum, laughing out loud at the traditional words of nomination.

Events would prove Kennedy lucky to have withdrawn from presidential contention early. In August 1983, Robert Kennedy, Jr., was arrested for possession of a gram of heroin. Revelations of drug use by a younger generation of Kennedys culminated in April 1984 in the death of David Kennedy from an overdose of cocaine, prescription pain killers and tranquilizers at a hotel in Palm Beach.

Senator Kennedy telephoned authorities to request the body of his nephew be removed so the investigation could be conducted in a less public setting. But this was Florida, not Massachusetts. Efforts to suppress information about the case didn't work. A court suit filed by a trio of newspapers sprung impounded records that revealed Caroline Kennedy to have visited the hotel 90 minutes before the body was discovered. Traces of drugs found in the room's toilet suggested efforts had been made to dispose of incriminating evidence—a "pure assumption," Herbert Miller said. Miller, the "shadow" counsellor of Chappaquiddick, was identified as a "Washington lawyer who represented the Kennedy family." A Miller-prepared statement over Caroline Kennedy's name denying she had entered the hotel room was released through Senator Kennedy's Washington office.

Kennedy kept a low profile until after the elections.

In December 1984, Kennedy made a highly publicized trip to Ethiopia to investigate famine conditions; then to South Africa on a fact-finding mission to study the racial problems of apartheid.

Accused of interfering in South Africa's internal affairs and exploiting a campaign-style barnstorming tour to launch his candidacy for the presidency in 1988, *The Financial Times* put Kennedy on its cover with the headline: "He's Teaching Us Morals?" An editorial inside, recalled the accident at Chappaquiddick in which a young woman had died in his car.

Kennedy was "seriously considering" running for President, an aide confirmed. "He's going to make a decision some time in the second half of 1985." Kennedy had made it clear, "I want very much to be President. I know I can make a difference."

By July 1985, Kennedy was leading all presidential preference polls. He "still must overcome the 16-year shadow of Chappaquiddick," but it was though he had turned his "negatives" around. The character issue would rise again, but the "saliency" of Chappaquiddick had diminished since 1979 in the view of advisers. The Senator had reached a point, "Where enough people will take a look at him on the basis of his record and values to elect him," *The New Republic* reported. Kennedy's staff had been instructed "to assume there will be a presidential campaign and prepare for it."

But a *Boston Globe* survey of Democratic state chairmen offered little encouragement to a Kennedy candidacy. One chairman observed, "The Chappaquiddick situation will just kill him as far as ever being elected president. You just hear it on the street. People still remember."

Any mention of a Kennedy candidacy was sufficient to evoke the issue. Despite his lead in the polls, a Kennedy candidacy would be suicidal. Kennedy could expect "some guy in a frogman outfit carrying a sign" at every political rally. Opponents needed only to point out, "They were too high-minded to raise the Chappaquiddick issue, central to the judgment of a man's character though it may be," to devastate his candidacy. For the first time, Kennedy would have to give up his Senate seat to seek the presidency. A loss would mean oblivion.

On December 19, 1985, Kennedy produced a video, and purchased time on two Boston television stations to announce his intention not to run for president in 1988. A grave Kennedy addressed the camera in a manner reminiscent of his Chappaquiddick speech to announce, "I know that this decision means that I may never be president. But the pursuit of the presidency is not my life. Public service is."

For sixteen years, the ghost of Chappaquiddick had hovered over his career, resisting all efforts to persuade the public that the real story had been told. Lodged in the nation's memory, the legacy of Chappaquiddick had concretized into a monument beneath which Kennedy was burying his presidential hopes. No historian, but a poet could inscribe the epitaph for the death of the Kennedy dream:

> Chappaquiddick, Chappaquiddick
> Your syllables echo the sea
> Your rhythm caught the vulnerable note—
> Shattered the walls of a dynasty.

* See Appendix 3